English Section C
Units 3 & 4

First published in 2024
Insight Publications Pty Ltd
3/350 Charman Road
Cheltenham Victoria 3192
Australia

Tel: +61 3 8571 4950
Email: books@insightpublications.com.au

www.insightpublications.com.au

Insight VCE Revision Questions: English Section C Units 3 & 4

ISBN: 9781923154957

Cover by Melisa Paredes
Internal design by Bec Yule @ Red Chilli Design
Layout by Melisa Paredes
Proofread by Janice Bird
Printed by Markono Print Media Pte Ltd

Insight Publications acknowledges the Traditional Custodians of the Country on which we meet and work, the Boonwurrung People of the Kulin Nation. We pay our respects to their Elders past and present, and extend that respect to all Aboriginal and Torres Strait Islander peoples.

Contents

Introduction

This *VCE Revision Questions: English Section C Units 3 & 4* resource contains a variety of scenarios consisting of persuasive media texts in different forms, together with background information about the text and the issue it addresses, similar to those you will encounter in the end-of-Year-12 English examination. Tips for analysing each scenario are also included. The second section of this resource presents a high-level sample analysis of each scenario. This resource complies with the 2024–2027 VCE English Study Design.

By using *VCE Revision Questions: English Section C Units 3 & 4* as part of your study regime throughout the year, you will be well prepared for the sorts of texts you may encounter in Section C of your end-of-year VCE English examination.

We wish you well with your studies.

The Insight Team

SCENARIOS

Scenario 1: Life skills in schools

Instructions

- In this section, you are required to analyse the use of argument(s) and language to persuade an intended audience to share the point of view expressed in an unseen persuasive text.
- Read the background information on this page and the material on the following pages, and write an analytical response to the task below.
- For the purposes of this task, the term 'language' refers to written and spoken language, and 'visuals' refers to images and graphics.
- This section is worth one-third of the total marks for the examination.

Task

Write an analysis of the ways in which argument(s), written and spoken language, and visuals are used in the material on the following pages to try to persuade the intended audience to share the point of view presented.

Background information

The Student Representative Council at Olympus High School has written an open letter to be circulated among Olympus High students, asking them to sign a petition. The council is seeking support from the student body to present the petition to the school board, requesting that dedicated classes on life skills be introduced at the school for students in Years 7–10.

Olympus High Student Representative Council needs your help!

Please sign our petition to show your support for the idea of dedicated life skills classes for Year 7–10 students.

Fellow students, something is wrong with our school system. Something is wrong when students know Pythagoras' theorem but don't know how to lodge a tax return. Something is wrong when students know that the mitochondria are the powerhouses of the cell but don't know how to manage conflict in their personal lives. The steps to the Nutbush might be handy to know at weddings, but surely mindfulness strategies and ways to cope with stress would be handier to know as we make the transition from adolescence to adulthood.

Our teaching and learning program should be focusing on the skills we need to succeed, not only in the professional world but also in our personal lives, and the government agrees. Personal and social capability is part of the Australian Curriculum. Across all year levels and studies, it is expected that students will develop skills in self-management and relationship-building. Such skills are designed to support students in becoming individuals who, as outlined in the Alice Springs (Mparntwe) Education Declaration agreed on by all Australian Education Ministers, can 'manage their emotional, mental, cultural, spiritual and physical wellbeing', have 'a sense of optimism about their lives' and can 'form and maintain healthy relationships'. The government recognises the importance of developing both resilience and the capacity for positive relationship-building in the next generation, so why doesn't Olympus High?

The expectation is that these skills will be taught across all study areas, but this is not happening. The school seems to think that setting group projects in science classes is enough to help us develop our communication and goal-setting skills, and that reading other people's work in history and English classes is enough to help us to develop empathy. But this is not enough. The Student Representative Council proposes that at least once per month a dedicated class be held focusing on the practical applications of these skills. The classes would be open to all students across Years 7–10 and could be held at lunchtime if scheduling proved an issue.

Each class would be led by a teacher from a different study area. We would have arts and music classes that focus on mental, emotional and spiritual wellbeing and mindfulness. We would have mathematics classes devoted to financial literacy and budgeting. We would have health and physical education classes focused on physical activity as a form of stress relief.

Providing students with practical strategies for dealing with stress and anxiety, in particular, should be a priority for our school leaders. The latest youth mental health report from Mission Australia and the Black Dog Institute found that, in the last seven years, psychological distress has risen by 5.5% among young people, and almost one in four young people in this country is experiencing mental health challenges. There is hope, however. According to research conducted by the Black Dog Institute, over 75% of mental health issues develop before the age of 25, indicating that early intervention is key. These classes would therefore be an investment in our long-term mental and emotional wellbeing.

Parents also agree that life skills should be taught in school. A 2019 study undertaken by Deana Leahy and Neil Selwyn of Monash University showed that parents want their children to receive a more holistic education. Responses to the question 'What new learning areas do people think should be taught in public schools?' referenced money management, home loans and taxes; job preparation such as résumé writing and interviewing; domestic tasks such as laundry and cooking; and conflict de-escalation.

While some may argue that these are skills we should be learning at home from our parents, it must be remembered that modern-day economic pressures mean that both parents are likely to be working full time. According to the Australian Bureau of Statistics, in over half of Australia's two-parent households, both parents worked full time in 2020. Parents' roles and responsibilities have changed in recent times, but our school system has not kept up. Our parents need support in passing on the skills necessary for us to thrive in the adult world.

So please, if you agree that Olympus students deserve to be given the best possible opportunity to succeed after high school, sign our petition and ask your parents to do so too. The school board meets next month. Let's try to get at least 100 signatures!

Tips

- The exclamatory headline aims to immediately catch readers' attention and position them to feel that they have something of value to offer in this debate, encouraging them to read on. Look for ways in which this kind of direct appeal is continued in the body of the text.
- Consider the text type – a petition – and intended audience – the writer's fellow students. The use of direct address – 'you' – and inclusive language – 'us', 'our' – aims to emphasise the shared interests of the writer and readers in order to get them on side.
- Humour is also used to engage the audience; for example in the reference to 'the steps to the Nutbush', and the image of shapes, which is reminiscent of shareable online memes. These would be familiar to students, helping them to feel that the issue is relevant to their lives and that engaging with it will be as easy as their everyday interactions on social media.
- Note that these humorous elements appear early in the piece, to develop a rapport with the reader from the beginning. Having done so, the writer shifts to a more serious tone to present evidence and research.
- The text opens and closes with a statement that directly addresses readers. Bookending the open letter with calls to action helps to create a sense of urgency in relation to the issue and positions readers to feel that they can and should act to support a change at their school.

Scenario 2: Greenwashing

Instructions

- In this section, you are required to analyse the use of argument(s) and language to persuade an intended audience to share the point of view expressed in an unseen persuasive text.
- Read the background information on this page and the material on the following pages, and write an analytical response to the task below.
- For the purposes of this task, the term 'language' refers to written and spoken language, and 'visuals' refers to images and graphics.
- This section is worth one-third of the total marks for the examination.

Task

Write an analysis of the ways in which argument(s), written and spoken language, and visuals are used in the material on the following pages to try to persuade the intended audience to share the point of view presented.

Background information

Makena Green-Moore is an environmental shopper and ethical consumerism advocate. The following is a transcript of her presentation at an expo on ethical consumerism. The presentation was accompanied by supporting images, and two of these images are included with the transcript.

Hello everyone. It is my great pleasure to welcome you all to today's presentation on ethical consumerism. Thank you so much for being here.

First, I would like to acknowledge the Wurundjeri People of the Kulin Nation as the Traditional Owners of the land we are meeting on. I would like to pay my respects to the Elders, past and present.

To get us started I'd like everyone to close their eyes and picture this: you are in the supermarket, and you need to buy a new shampoo. While perusing the rack you see that a big sticker has been added to the front of an already familiar bottle: 'ALL NATURAL INGREDIENTS'. Fantastic, you think: now you can satisfy your need for shampoo and also buy something great for the environment.

WRONG!

You have just been subjected to 'greenwashing' or 'green sheen': an unethical marketing strategy designed to make you believe you are buying an eco-conscious product, when actually the company is not putting in the money, time and effort to create something environmentally friendly.

Greenwashing can take many forms, and specialised language has been created by clever manufacturers and marketers to convince consumers that they are making a more ethical choice than they truly are.

'All natural' is a common phrase thrown around by greenwashing marketers. This vague term implies an eco-friendliness without actually having to deliver on making a product environmentally beneficial. Think about it: most things are naturally occurring in some way, but that doesn't necessarily mean that they are good for you or good for the planet. Other terms often used include 'non-toxic', 'raw' and 'plant-based'. Not one of these descriptions guarantees that the product benefits or avoids harming the environment in any way. Some companies have also created false labels or symbols that imply that they care about our cause. For example, a small green flower positioned on the bottom of the label can look deceptively similar to the real and well-known symbols that denote products being cruelty-free and recyclable.

The great news is that many of the companies who are well known for greenwashing are being called out and held accountable.

The Earth Island Institute recently filed a lawsuit against Coca-Cola for falsely advertising its products as eco-friendly while this company remains the largest plastic polluter in the world. The lawsuit was a retaliation against Coke's revelation that the bottles were being made with 'plant plastic' – an announcement attempting to sell the idea that the packaging would break down more easily than ever before. However, this misses the point entirely. Plant-based plastic is still plastic, and it is an unnecessary product when the more sustainable alternatives of glass and aluminium already exist.

Beware the label – a popular form of greenwashing.

What's great about this is that Coca-Cola is already being taken to court over its misleading marketing, and now there will be real pressure on the company to genuinely reduce the environmental impact of its packaging.

Of course, that is an example of dealing with greenwashing on a large and extremely expensive scale – not all of us can afford to take on a giant company in a legal battle.

So, what easy changes can we make to our own shopping habits to ensure we aren't falling for these nasty tactics?

As I mentioned earlier, pay careful attention to the terminology being used on packaging; think about what terms like 'all natural' really mean, and ensure you know what the real eco-friendly symbols look like. Pictures of nature, greenery and flowers will often be used but do not represent official approval. If you are concerned that the producers of your favourite products aren't being honest with you, reach out to them and ask for the truth. You can find the contact details for brands online, so get in touch and tell them your concerns. If you get a vague response then they probably have nothing positive to say. It might be difficult to say goodbye to a much-loved favourite, but there are many great ethical products out there for you to try.

If you can, try to buy local alternatives – a farmers' market is a great place to buy produce direct from the people who make it, usually with minimal or no packaging. Ultimately, with a little bit of extra knowledge, a keen eye and the will to do what is right, we can make many small changes in our lives that will all add up to a more environmentally friendly and sustainable community.

Thank you all again for your attendance today. I'll be around the expo for a while so please feel free to approach me if you have any questions about ethical consuming or greenwashing, or even if you'd just like to say hello. And remember – don't let the big corporations pull the wool over your eyes!

Tips

- In your analysis, it is especially important to take into account the context of this text. The speaker is addressing an audience of people she can assume to be receptive to her message, given their attendance at an ethical consumerism expo. She is thus able to take for granted their interest in caring for the environment and therefore focus on ways in which they can do this most effectively.
- The speaker repeatedly addresses the audience directly, using 'you'; this both retains her listeners' attention and helps her to foster a connection with them.
- Look for other ways in which the speaker aims to develop this connection – for example, through her invitation to 'please feel free to approach me', which helps to create an impression of friendliness and transparency.
- The inclusion of the Acknowledgement of Country at the beginning of the speech further reinforces the speaker's ethical credentials, contributing to an image of her as informed and concerned with social justice issues, an impression likely to be well received by a like-minded audience.
- Though the speaker's aim is to alert her audience to greenwashing tactics, she is careful not to put listeners offside by suggesting that they are foolish or ignorant to believe manufacturers' claims about environmental friendliness. By referring to 'clever' marketers and manufacturers, whose tactics are 'unethical' and 'nasty', she places the blame for greenwashing squarely on organisations, rather than on consumers themselves. This allows her audience to feel that her advice will give them an advantage when it comes to assessing companies' environmental claims, rather than positioning them to feel that they bear any guilt if they have previously fallen for the sorts of hollow claims she criticises.

Scenario 3: Highfield Markets

Instructions

- In this section, you are required to analyse the use of argument(s) and language to persuade an intended audience to share the point of view expressed in an unseen persuasive text.
- Read the background information on this page and the material on the following pages, and write an analytical response to the task below.
- For the purposes of this task, the term 'language' refers to written and spoken language, and 'visuals' refers to images and graphics.
- This section is worth one-third of the total marks for the examination.

Task

Write an analysis of the ways in which argument(s), written and spoken language, and visuals are used in the material on the following pages to try to persuade the intended audience to share the point of view presented.

Background information

Highfield Discussions is a podcast that addresses community issues in the Highfield area. In this episode, Ravi Nicholson expresses his views on the proposed loss of the local markets, with the intended replacement being a large supermarket. The transcript was published on the *Highfield Discussions* website, as well as on relevant social media platforms, accompanied by two images.

Hello to you all, I hope you're having a great day. You're probably wondering why you're hearing from me again so soon. I'm making this episode as a bit of a bonus feature; something has come to my attention, and I really couldn't sit on it until next week. I think, at this point, we all know how passionate I am about our community. Obviously, Highfield has seen a lot of change recently, and most of it has been fantastic. The new local pool is a great addition, I've loved the green spaces being used for morning yoga, and the street veggie patch has contributed to more than my fair share of meals. But … I was absolutely heartbroken to find out yesterday that there are talks of demolishing the Highfield Markets. I've been running around those stalls since I was five; it's always been such an open, safe space. As kids we would all duck and weave between stands, sheltering from the sun under colourful umbrellas before launching back into a new game. If we fell? Not to worry – plenty of friendly faces were around to provide a pat on the back, a bandaid and an icy pole for good measure. Even now as an adult I'm happy to say that my children run around just as we all did then. So, I got to thinking about the proposed demolition. Is it for a new structure? Are they revamping the markets? Are they moving them and making room for a new community feature?

I'll let you know now, it's none of the above. They want to demolish the markets to make room for a new supermarket. Just another chain store in a big concrete block. To me, and many others, this would be an unthinkable loss. I can understand it; our recent community upgrades make this a very desirable and well-serviced location and we have had an influx of new neighbours – which is great! I'm not surprised we have been put on the map, and if the developers had been able to find an empty space to fill, I don't think anyone would mind. But this comes at the cost of the families and small businesses that have worked out of and relied on these markets for decades. Our local economy is at stake; the work and wellbeing of beloved community members is being undermined. Even beyond this, the produce and goods that will be supplied by this supermarket won't be able to compare with the high-quality fresh products that we are used to.

I don't know about you, but I don't want another lifeless supermarket chain arriving at the expense of small businesses that provide our community with a heartbeat. Demolishing the markets threatens not only our local economy but also a core pillar of our community. So much of what makes Highfield special can be found at the markets. I couldn't imagine a Sunday morning without a coffee from Letitia's stand, fresh fruit from Manuel's, and Francois' fresh bread. It is these businesses – these people – who will suffer if this moves forward.

Ultimately, I care more about the livelihood of the families and their independent businesses than I do about the profit margins of a big developer. These supermarket chains clearly haven't considered the amount of community support for local enterprises. By shopping at the supermarket, we would be sending the profits outside of our community, giving the supermarkets money that they won't be putting back into our local economy. The markets are not only an economic backbone of our community, but also a social one, and I say this because I KNOW that Highfield is behind me.

To my listeners, I'm asking you to consider what you can do to keep Highfield safe. Many of you will already have seen the protest posters and signs around the markets and I applaud those who created these for taking action so quickly. I also have the 'Protect Highfield Markets' petition link in the episode description, and I would really love to see more people throw their weight behind this important issue. Write to your local councillor and make your feelings known.

Most of all, head down to the markets this weekend and every weekend and support the businesses that are still there. Each one of them desperately needs us to demonstrate how essential they are to our community. You can do this while also getting some great produce. Highfield is a community that cares for each other during the hard times, so please support what makes us special and protest against what will make us ordinary.

Next week we will be back to our regular programming, so thanks for listening and remember to shop local!

Tips

- Consider how the opening of the text primes listeners to view the issue as both urgent and relevant, as the speaker makes the point that this is a 'bonus feature' that he couldn't 'sit on' for another week. This opening also treats listeners as a community that is well acquainted with the podcast and its host, strengthening a pre-existing rapport.
- Note the way in which the two images are intended to work in tandem by presenting two starkly contrasting views of the market site – one in which the area is bustling and vibrant, and one in which it is almost empty and seems desolate. This contrast reinforces the one conveyed in the spoken text, between the popular markets that foster a sense of community and the proposed supermarket development that the speaker argues will undermine it.
- The speaker repeatedly frames the supermarket development as a threat through careful language choices with connotations of harm and destruction, such as 'demolish', 'lifeless' and 'suffer'. Look for other examples, and consider the emotions being targeted by this vocabulary.
- Contrast these negative vocabulary choices with the descriptions of the current markets – e.g. 'open', 'safe', 'high-quality fresh products', 'heartbeat'. Such choices work to establish the market as vital to the community, positioning listeners to feel that the proposed development threatens not only a familiar place to shop but their wellbeing and safety, as well as their sense of community.
- Consider the way Nicholson creates a connection with his audience by repeatedly addressing them directly throughout his podcast. The medium of the podcast allows the speaker to build this sort of rapport with his audience, and the use of direct address also helps him to personalise the issue.

Scenario 4: Handwriting

Instructions

- In this section, you are required to analyse the use of argument(s) and language to persuade an intended audience to share the point of view expressed in an unseen persuasive text.
- Read the background information on this page and the material on the following pages, and write an analytical response to the task below.
- For the purposes of this task, the term 'language' refers to written and spoken language, and 'visuals' refers to images and graphics.
- This section is worth one-third of the total marks for the examination.

Task

Write an analysis of the ways in which argument(s), written and spoken language, and visuals are used in the material on the following pages to try to persuade the intended audience to share the point of view presented.

Background information

The following opinion piece by Leslie Slater appeared in a magazine supplement to a weekend newspaper. It is her response to discussions about the increasing use of computer technology, particularly in education, and the implications for handwriting.

The vanishing art of handwriting

By Leslie Slater

It was only a couple of years ago that I discovered the pleasures of using a fountain pen. The way each stroke of a letter can be subtly varied, depending on the angle and pressure with which the nib is placed on the page. The way the colour of the ink gradually changes as it dries. And yes, the way the letters smudge if my hand rests on the drying ink: a sign of imperfection and vulnerability; a mirror held up to their human creator. From being a purely functional task, writing has now taken on a more creative quality, and I have an enhanced awareness of how the *content* of writing is intertwined with the *process*.

Then there are the environmental benefits: no more disposable pens going into landfill. A bottle of ink lasts a long time, and the glass can be recycled. Even the refill process has its own ritualistic elements, as the pen is first flushed carefully with water and then ink is drawn up with a few turns of the converter. The variety of ink colours available is far greater than the narrow range of stock-standard colours in disposable pens, encompassing shades of pink, amber, coffee, grey, violet and everything in between.

Beautiful handwriting: a vanishing art?

Nor am I alone in appreciating the act of handwriting, especially (though not exclusively) with bottled ink and fountain pen. The book *The Missing Ink: The Lost Art of Handwriting (and Why it Still Matters)* by Philip Hensher also celebrates the pleasures of handwriting. For Hensher, handwriting is not just a means of conveying information, but an expression of the individual that incorporates 'a little bit of their personality into the form of their message'. In other words, handwriting is essentially personal and unique rather than mechanical and mass-produced.

Yet at this moment in history, the future of handwriting is suddenly extremely uncertain. As Hensher admits, he wrote his book at a time 'when, it seems, handwriting is about to vanish from our lives altogether'. Computers, tablets and smart phones mean we are, as never before, finger-tapping at keyboards and keypads rather than deliberately shaping each stroke and curve of letters and punctuation marks. For a culture to lose handwriting is, perhaps, also to lose part of its history, its identity, even its humanity.

Of course, handwriting is still taught in Australian primary schools. But typing on laptops and other devices is the vastly more common way in which students produce written work, meaning that secondary school students are left to find their own preferred way of handwriting – on the rare occasions when they still need to. Then they somehow have to overcome the challenge of writing their exams, which can be up to three hours long in Year 12. Experienced English and Literature teacher Kim Jones notes that many senior students resort to printing and even block capital letters, which can mean they struggle in a written exam. 'Some students find it too physically difficult as the muscles in their hands and fingers become sore and fatigued. They don't write as much as they should and they may fail to complete all their answers.' It seems just a matter of time before all exams will be undertaken electronically. Once that happens there will be little or no reason for students to handwrite beyond their early primary school years, with the resulting loss of those skills acquired in the first 11 or 12 years of life. The writing, as they say, is on the wall.

Is it only old-fashioned types like me who will mourn the loss of handwriting? Is it just about aesthetics – about something *looking* beautiful, but lacking much use or meaning? Or an empty nostalgia about how it was in the 'old days'? And anyway, what exactly *does* poor or immaculate handwriting say about the individual – about, for instance, their personal qualities or values? We don't make assumptions about someone's personality purely on the basis of their skill in athletics or ball sports. Perhaps handwriting says nothing much at all about us, and doing it much less, or not at all, in no way compromises our intelligence or our humanity.

Students almost exclusively complete assignments electronically nowadays.

Yet there is a growing body of evidence that suggests we do, somehow, think *differently*, and perhaps *better*, when we handwrite than when we type. In a US study reported on the University of Washington website, professor of educational psychology Virginia Berninger and her colleagues compared how 200 students in grades 2, 4 and 6 completed writing tasks using a pen and using a keyboard. 'Children consistently did better writing with a pen when they wrote essays,' says Berninger. 'They wrote more and they wrote faster.' Although it is far from clear why this might be, Berninger suggests that 'a keyboard doesn't allow a child to have the same opportunity to engage the hand while forming letters – on a keyboard a letter is selected by pressing a key and is not formed'. She adds, 'brain imaging studies with adults have shown an advantage for forming letters over selecting or viewing letters'.

Another study found that adults learning a new (foreign) alphabet by hand scored better in recognition tests than those learning the alphabet using a keyboard and screen. When brain scans were performed, those who learned by hand showed more activity in the part of the brain that controls language comprehension. In other words, the way we write affects the way we learn. And the way we learn affects … well, just about everything.

All of which suggests it's far too early to be complacent about the shift away from pen and paper. What gifts handwriting may have for us may not be fully understood until it's too late – when handwriting is no longer part of the curriculum (as in many states in the US), and when teachers lack the knowledge of how to teach it because they haven't learned it themselves. The information age is here, and it's essentially a digital, computer age with great liberating and democratic potential. But that doesn't mean that we can't also keep what's valuable, unique and often beautiful from the past. Handwriting is not only a vital part of our heritage; it may also be a crucial part of our minds.

Tips

- Note the way in which Slater balances emotional appeals to aesthetics and nostalgia with logical, evidence-based arguments regarding the usefulness of handwriting to memory and learning. How might this help her appeal to a wide and diverse audience?
- Slater bolsters her argument with references to expert testimony; these are varied yet all relevant to the field of education, thus providing strong evidence in support of her opinion. Referring to both Australian and international evidence implies that the writer's research is wide-ranging and her conclusions thus more reliable. It also suggests that the issue is of global significance, inclining the reader to feel that something important is at stake.
- The writer uses an often lyrical tone, particularly in the opening and closing paragraphs. Identify particular language choices that contribute to this tone and reflect on how it supports her two-pronged argument about the value of handwriting.
- Consider the importance of the place of publication of this piece. Its appearance in a supplementary weekend magazine means that readers are likely to consume it in a more leisurely, thoughtful way than they might a piece published in the main daily news section of the newspaper. Thus the writer's considered meditations on the issue are likely to be received in a similarly considered manner by her audience.
- Note the two images included with the article: the first, a close-up of a handwritten note, illustrates the writer's view regarding the beauty of handwriting. The image centres on a sleek fountain pen which, in tandem with the caption, encourages readers to see for themselves the beauty of traditional handwriting. The second is framed from a first-person perspective, which attempts to manoeuvre the reader to situate themselves in the position of the student. The crumpled paper represents the metaphorical discarding of physical implements such as pen and paper, and suggests a sense of frustration compared to the emphasis on beauty in the first image.

Scenario 5: Penny's Petals

Instructions

- In this section, you are required to analyse the use of argument(s) and language to persuade an intended audience to share the point of view expressed in an unseen persuasive text.
- Read the background information on this page and the material on the following pages, and write an analytical response to the task below.
- For the purposes of this task, the term 'language' refers to written and spoken language, and 'visuals' refers to images and graphics.
- This section is worth one-third of the total marks for the examination.

Task

Write an analysis of the ways in which argument(s), written and spoken language, and visuals are used in the material on the following pages to try to persuade the intended audience to share the point of view presented.

Background information

Penelope Acosta is the owner of the local flower shop Penny's Petals. She has written a blog post about what inspired her to start her business, and the ethics of the modern cut-flower business. She has shared this post on her social media pages.

Shock in the Shop! The Ethics of Cut Flowers

By Penelope Acosta

A rose by any other name would smell as sweet – but where did that rose come from?

This was the question I asked myself ten years ago when receiving a beautiful bouquet for my 30th birthday. Roses were far and away my favourite flower, but surely it was the wrong time of year for such a gorgeous display. How were these flowers able to bloom in autumn?

Thus, my search started, and I was shocked to find out that the roses I so adored had a far more sinister background than I ever could have imagined.

The modern flower industry is fraught with difficulty, exploitation and environmentally dangerous practices. With the global cut-flower industry being worth an estimated US$55 billion, the majority of flowers are being imported from South America and East Asia. Colombia leads all other flower producers, having sold 660 million stems during 2020. The plants on these flower farms are grown in industrial-scale greenhouses that can occupy more than 200 hectares. Here the workers can be expected to work 16-hour days.

Further, although floriculture exposes workers to fertilisers, insecticides and preservatives that are absolutely full of toxins, employees are often expected to work without personal protective equipment. Despite taking these risks, the workers are paid far below the minimum wage, hardly able to support themselves and their families.

Just when I thought this couldn't get worse, I found that it is not only the workers who are affected, but also the communities surrounding these unscrupulous flower farms. In Ecuador, young children who come into contact with floriculture workers have been found to have altered short-term brain activity that is suspected to be a result of contamination from pesticide residue on clothes and equipment.

Everything I have mentioned so far is shocking enough, but it doesn't even consider the environmental toll this industry can take. The masses of stems being grown on flower farms need vast quantities of water, putting a huge strain on local resources. Once these flowers have been harvested, they are distributed all over the world, leaving an astronomical carbon footprint in their wake. Finally, once in store at the florist or supermarket, they are wrapped in harsh plastics and shoved onto foam blocks that are laced with chemicals and virtually impossible to recycle or dispose of ethically.

I couldn't see how I could keep enjoying a birthday bouquet with all of this new knowledge. How could I be sure that the flowers I was buying were ethically sourced and sustainably grown?

So, I started my own florist shop. Ten years on, I am proud to say that the flowers I sell at Penny's Petals aren't grown using any of these questionable methods, and anyone buying from our shop can rest assured that I take the greatest care with my work.

My first intention with every bloom is to attempt to grow it myself. I have a small local farm, where I grow my beautiful Australian natives. I also have a greenhouse that I use for my harder-to-grow crops – but I take care not to overuse water or chemicals. My family and I carefully attend to each and every plant, using only the most eco-friendly and sustainable of products.

If I can't find a way to produce the flowers myself, I make the effort to source my flowers from Aussie farmers, who I know take the time to nurture strong and beautiful plants while minimising the use of water and toxic chemicals. I also have the added pleasure of supporting Australian businesses just like mine. Penny's Petals doesn't use foam blocks or plastics; we wrap our flowers in recyclable materials and, where possible, we supply a second-hand vase to keep your beautiful arrangements blooming for longer.

The next time you are in a mad dash to impress, or say sorry, or buy that 'just because' bouquet, forget the big chains. Sure, they might save you a few dollars, but you are overlooking the real cost of those stems.

Tips

- » Be alert to the dual purpose of the blog post – to dissuade the reader from purchasing flowers that are not ethically produced and to promote the writer's own florist business in order to increase sales.
- » This double purpose leads Acosta to create a dichotomy between irresponsible, unethical 'big chain' flower-sellers on the one hand and ethical business on the other. Note, however, that the ethical practices she describes all relate to her own business, thus implying that the best or only option for the responsible consumer is to purchase from Penny's Petals.
- » Acosta makes frequent use of highly emotive language, such as 'shocking', 'dangerous' and 'sinister', which work together to develop a strongly negative portrayal of traditional florists and aim to evoke fear, sympathy and outrage in the reader.
- » She also uses extreme language, such as 'astronomical' and 'virtually impossible', which intensifies her use of emotive terms to convey an impression of the situation as dire and therefore requiring urgent action.
- » Throughout the piece, Acosta frequently alludes to her personal knowledge of and interactions with the florist industry. She attempts to portray herself as an expert with extensive experience relevant to the topic. She also attempts to frame herself as an unsuspecting victim of unethical business practices, further lending her credibility as someone who has been exposed to the modern flower industry's issues. Consider how the context of the post's publication (on Acosta's social media and blog) might make her target audience more likely to accept her claims of authority.

Scenario 6: The wearable workplace

Instructions

- In this section, you are required to analyse the use of argument(s) and language to persuade an intended audience to share the point of view expressed in an unseen persuasive text.
- Read the background information on this page and the material on the following pages, and write an analytical response to the task below.
- For the purposes of this task, the term ‘language’ refers to written and spoken language, and ‘visuals’ refers to images and graphics.
- This section is worth one-third of the total marks for the examination.

Task

Write an analysis of the ways in which argument(s), written and spoken language, and visuals are used in the material on the following pages to try to persuade the intended audience to share the point of view presented.

Background information

The article below was published in *SuitNoTie*, an online publication for business executives who want to keep up with the latest trends and developments in the business world. Forsythe is a staff writer at *SuitNoTie* and he is the former CEO of a multinational company.

The wearable workplace

By Brannigan Forsythe

It's official – the wearable technology revolution is here, and there's plenty of room for businesses to get in on the action. From managing employee health to improving overall productivity, companies around the globe are using wearables to supercharge their operations, and there's no reason you can't do the same. Curious? We show you why now is the time to start thinking about working wearables into your world.

You can't put a price on health – or can you?

A quick survey of wearable tech on the market right now will tell you two things: one, wearables are more popular than ever; and two, they're predominantly pitched at the health conscious (or those trying to be).

It might be a little hard to see the angle here, at least at first glance. Being health-conscious – getting your steps in, measuring the distance you run each morning – is great, but what does that have to do with you and your business?

There are plenty of reasons why health and fitness should be a company concern as well as a personal one. Research tells us that fitter and healthier employees have higher energy levels, are less likely to get sick and are more productive in the long term.

But getting your workers to take responsibility for improving their health is not so easy, especially as many employers are reluctant to order their employees to do so.

Enter wearables. As many companies can tell you, encouraging employees to use wearable tech like a Fitbit is a great way to foster greater health consciousness in your workplace, and the cost for the company is relatively small.

After all, what would you prefer to be paying for? A fitness tracker – which is getting cheaper by the day – or the cost of covering sick leave?

Wearables that work for you

Sickness and injury are simply an unpleasant reality that workplaces have to deal with, but there's no doubt that the incidence can vary from industry to industry.

When it comes to retail and manufacturing, the risk (and cost) can be crippling. US insurance company Liberty Mutual estimated the direct cost of overexertion injuries in these areas to be US$15.1 billion (one-quarter of the total workplace injury direct costs), and there's no reason to think that the proportion of costs in Australia would be significantly different.

Would activity trackers stop your workers getting injured on the job? Probably not, but there are a range of other wearable options out there – with some very impressive applications.

Step inside an Audi assembly plant, for example, and you'll be greeted by some of the world's first bionic workers. The German car maker has been trialling the use of wearable exoskeletons to reduce the stress on workers' bodies. Worn like a piece of clothing, the exoskeleton connects at the hips and features support structures across specific points on the upper and lower body.

Wearables also offer a number of benefits when it comes to responding to on-the-job accidents. Though not as complex as an exoskeleton, tech like Wearsafe is set to dramatically improve safety in high-risk environments.

Wearsafe is a wearable tag that can be activated with the push of a button in an emergency, automatically contacting first responders and supervisors with location data and real-time audio from the incident. It's a deceptively simple tech solution to an age-old problem – knowing where your workers are, what they're doing and when they get into trouble – and another example of wearable tech's revolutionary potential.

But there's more to this picture than physical fitness and safety. As any human resources manager will tell you, poor mental health is just as much of a drain on productivity as physical injury. The problem for those in management, however, is how to identify mental health issues early on.

Well, good news, folks! There's a wearable for that.

Take a look at multinational company Hitachi, which has been trialling wearable sensors that collect and analyse data on employee behaviour to improve happiness. The state-of-the-art tech, embedded into what looks like a regular worker ID, tracks an employee's activities throughout the day to measure their levels of job satisfaction. The data is then analysed to highlight areas that management can improve upon to keep workers happy and, therefore, more productive.

Hitachi is not alone. Companies all over the world are using similar tech to measure employees' heart rates, as well as their fatigue and stress levels, to determine when they might be in need of a break (or a little more incentive!).

Working out what fits (and wearing the consequences)

Okay, you might now be convinced about the value of bringing wearables into the workplace, but be warned – it's not going to be such an easy sell to your employees.

With privacy concerns around technology use a high priority for many people, the prospect of employers collecting data on workers is likely to be met with some resistance. A recent survey by PricewaterhouseCoopers found that 82 per cent of respondents were concerned about the privacy implications of wearable tech, with many voicing concerns about the kinds of data collected, who would have access to it and what it might be used for.

The real issue, then, is trust, and the decision to implement wearable tech should come with a comprehensive plan for educating employees about how they will be affected and what processes are in place to protect their information.

That being said, it's clear that wearables are here to stay (they're not wearing out!), and keen CEOs need to keep ahead of the curve – lest they watch the revolution pass them by.

Forsythe is a staff writer at SuitNoTie and the former CEO of a multinational company.

Tips

- Consider how the identity of the writer of the opinion piece might affect the way in which the audience responds to his point of view. The credit line suggests that he is experienced and knowledgeable in the field, inclining the reader to trust his opinion. This authoritative status is also suggested by his use of statistics and references to high-profile multinational companies in his examples.
- Consider how the predominant tone of the article is likely to affect the audience. It is upbeat and positive, and reflects a professionalism appropriate to the context in which the piece appears. This is intended to evoke feelings of trust and positivity in the audience, which is likely to consist of fellow businesspeople eager to find out about ways to increase productivity in their workplaces. Appealing to their desire to be modern and up to date, the writer uses motivational expressions such as 'keep ahead of the curve' with which such readers are likely to be familiar and to find compelling.
- The structure of the piece further caters to the specific target audience with the inclusion of subheadings that highlight key points for readers who might not have the time or inclination to read the text from start to finish. It is also reminiscent of the structure of a workplace report of the sort readers are likely to be familiar with, and inclined to view as reliable and meaningful.
- Analyse the way the image presents an alternative viewpoint to that expressed in the opinion piece in order to rebut it. The cartoon depicts an employee who is clearly stressed, as indicated by the beads of sweat around his face as he runs. His wearable device is telling him that he is fired, which might be read as suggesting that such technology has excessive power over employees' lives. However, the exaggerated and comical nature of the illustration, together with the context of its appearance with the written piece undercuts any alarm the image might evoke. Rather the unlikelihood of an employee being fired by a wearable device operates to convey the idea that concern about wearable devices in the workplace is exaggerated and even ridiculous.

Scenario 7: Halloween

Instructions

- In this section, you are required to analyse the use of argument(s) and language to persuade an intended audience to share the point of view expressed in an unseen persuasive text.
- Read the background information on this page and the material on the following pages, and write an analytical response to the task below.
- For the purposes of this task, the term 'language' refers to written and spoken language, and 'visuals' refers to images and graphics.
- This section is worth one-third of the total marks for the examination.

Task

Write an analysis of the ways in which argument(s), written and spoken language, and visuals are used in the material on the following pages to try to persuade the intended audience to share the point of view presented.

Background information

The *Redfern Reader*, a free suburban newspaper, has a regular opinion column for members of the community to share their thoughts on local events. Recently there has been an influx of letters about Halloween and trick-or-treating. Local Redfern resident Nadia Laghari has written an opinion piece for the column, sharing her thoughts on the celebration.

Halloween – treat or trick? A personal journey

By Nadia Laghari

Well, it's that time of year again. Decorations are popping up everywhere, pumpkins are appearing in front yards (and in the veggie aisle!) and the kids seem to be more excited with every day. It's too early for Christmas, and we've just had school holidays – it must be Halloween.

It's taken me a long time to understand why we bother with Halloween. We already have so much American influence in our culture – movies, TV shows, music – without adopting one of their celebrations as well. I've often thought I'd prefer some kind of Australian festival on that day, rather than something with no local relevance. And as it stands, I don't love a ritual centred on the mass consumption of lollies. It's hard enough to encourage my kids to eat healthily without this sugary occasion on the calendar. Not to mention the havoc it brings to the dinnertime schedule. Halloween frequently falls on a school night, and dinner and bedtime are put on hold until whenever the kids are back from trick-or-treating. There's also the need to juggle getting the older kids to and from sports training, and running to the door every few minutes to dole out lollies to a never-ending stream of strangers. Then there are the yearly demands for new plastic costumes that just end up in the back of the cupboard, or even in the bin. While I would hate my kids to feel left out because they're not dressed in a great outfit, the thought of so much waste makes my head spin.

These used to be my first thoughts each October as I dreaded that haunted night. But over the years, seeing how much fun the kids have in their costumes with their friends, the life it brings to the street, and, yes, even sneaking a few lollies throughout the night myself, has gradually encouraged me to rethink Halloween. It didn't happen overnight, but by making an effort and getting more involved, I now find that I don't just tolerate Halloween – I enjoy it.

Seeing how the community makes Halloween its own on 31 October, I've grown to like the occasion. Plastic-wrapped candy is often replaced with home-baked cookies and fruit from the community garden. We've taken to giving out trail mix (trick 'n' mix!) pouches, to try and strike a balance of naughty and nice. We get a chance to say hello to neighbours we've fallen out of touch with, and meet the new families who have made this suburb their home in the past year. Seeing the street come to life with kids and adults alike dressed up and laughing has become a real highlight of my year. While we sometimes have street parties or get-togethers at other times, an event that includes the whole suburb feels really special.

It's also given me a chance to turn some of my worries into active opportunities to have fun with my kids, and even to impart some lessons. While, before, I might have been worried about their costumes being bought that morning and thrown away 24 hours later, now we see the costume challenge as an opportunity to imaginatively repurpose old clothes that might otherwise never get worn again. Not only does this give them a chance to actually practise reusing and recycling, it's creative and lets us bond over sticky tape and craft glue (no pun intended!). It's also a great opportunity to see what they've been reading and watching, and which characters they like enough to want to dress up as. It's even inspired me to participate – I have a bit of a costume in the works this year!

I used to push back against a celebration that was so clearly imported, but then, so are Christmas and Easter, and we certainly enjoy those. The calendar is full of rituals that didn't start here, and to celebrate them all is to celebrate the multicultural nature of Australia. Just as we go to the beach rather than play in the snow on Christmas morning, enjoying a warm spring night and making a community catch-up out of Halloween lets us put our own unique spin on the occasion.

Tips

- The writer devotes considerable space at the beginning of her piece to explaining the aspects of Halloween she once objected to. Consider how this primes readers, particularly those who might also feel negatively about Halloween, to be prepared to think differently about it, as the writer herself has come to do. It also serves to present the writer as open-minded and reasonable, since she is willing to change her thinking in the face of new evidence or ideas. This is likely to encourage readers to trust that her opinion will be logical and considered.
- The two images present different perspectives on Halloween, reinforcing the argument presented in the written text, which moves from detailing one viewpoint against Halloween to endorsing a contrasting viewpoint in favour of Halloween. The first image focuses on the excesses of the celebration, with an abundance of lollies carelessly spilling out of a large bucket. In light of the image's position within the text near the writer's reference to 'mass consumption of lollies', the reader is steered towards viewing this image negatively. However, the writer goes on to admit 'sneaking a few lollies', a confession intended to present her as relatable and also signalling a shift in her argument and her opinion of Halloween. As she goes on to outline its many benefits, reinforced by the second image of smiling, costumed children, the reader is prompted to reconsider the first image as one of innocent and understandable occasional indulgence.
- The second image helps to support this reframing by presenting happy children, possibly siblings, enjoying a shared experience. One child holds a bowl of lollies while the other two hold carved pumpkins, a reminder that the day is more about shared activities such as pumpkin-carving than it is about sugar consumption. The typical costumes worn by the three, together with these stereotypical Halloween props, convey the idea that this is the essence of the occasion – innocent fun and togetherness.
- Note the way in which the writer anticipates and gently rebuts a common argument against celebrating Halloween in Australia – that it is a custom imported from the United States. By acknowledging that she herself once shared this objection, reminding readers that other widely enjoyed customs are also imported, and asserting that they have the power to put their 'own unique spin' on Halloween, she encourages readers to reassess their preconceptions without compromising their belief in the importance of uniquely Australian traditions.

Scenario 8: The Salty Boot

Instructions

- In this section, you are required to analyse the use of argument(s) and language to persuade an intended audience to share the point of view expressed in an unseen persuasive text.
- Read the background information on this page and the material on the following pages, and write an analytical response to the task below.
- For the purposes of this task, the term 'language' refers to written and spoken language, and 'visuals' refers to images and graphics.
- This section is worth one-third of the total marks for the examination.

Task

Write an analysis of the ways in which argument(s), written and spoken language, and visuals are used in the material on the following pages to try to persuade the intended audience to share the point of view presented.

Background information

Iconic live-music venue The Salty Boot – colloquially known as 'the Boot' – is being forced to close down due to pressure from new local residents of the inner-city suburb of Metropolo in Melbourne. These new residents say the venue is too noisy and this has become a problem for the increasing number of people moving to the popular area. A group of musicians, music fans and longstanding local residents are campaigning against the closure. Vince D'Angelo, a local rock musician, is speaking at the campaign rally. The following is a transcript of his speech.

A flyer for the rally – created by cartoonist and long-time supporter of The Salty Boot, Roisin McCrae – is included at the end of the transcript.

Ladies, gentlemen, music fans.

It's with a heavy heart that I stand before you today.

Behind me is our beloved Salty Boot, which, if those naysayers and complainers get their way, will call last drinks this afternoon, and retire that old sound system.

The new gentrified neighbourhood we find ourselves in has spoken, and, by their thinking, The Salty Boot no longer fits with the suburb's trendy aesthetic, or its new reputation for quiet inner-city living. This is despite the fact that a recent survey by a renowned firm has indicated that the majority of people living in Metropolo, and over 80% of Melbourne residents, want the Boot to remain open.

The Salty Boot is too loud. It's too colourful. And, most offensive of all, it's too proud of it.

Come next week they'll start the process of changing this glorious building into a boutique hairdressing salon, a flat-pack furniture emporium or, more likely, a hip cafe.

And some might say, so what? A loud and filthy pub? Good riddance.

But they don't know this place like we do.

When I look at the dirty facade behind us, I see much more than a filthy pub – I see a home. And I know many of you feel the same way.

This is the place where I heard live rock-and-roll for the first time, played my first ever gig on a rusted bass guitar, ordered my first beer and spent many a night in the company of good friends. It was my refuge when things were tough, and the only place I ever felt like I could be who I wanted to be.

The Salty Boot, as any of you can attest, is a special place, full of life, love and, of course, great music, and it deserves to be preserved – for my sake, for yours and for this city's.

For the last 40 years, The Salty Boot has supported emerging artists. It welcomed us, and let us perform when no other entertainment venue would. Without the Boot, many of us, including myself and the internationally acclaimed musician Trombone Jackson, would not have become the famous and successful musicians we are today.

Say goodbye to the Boot, and we say goodbye to more than the building, or to chicken parmas that taste like tyre rubber.

Say goodbye to the Boot and we're one step closer to living in a world of cool nothingness, where band t-shirts belong on walls, where street art is commissioned for tidy sums and music is for working out to, rather than really *feeling*.

Say goodbye to the Boot and we're three-quarters of the way to boring, headed for Plainsville.

Where will people go to forget about the drudgery of everyday life, to bliss out to the sound of a soaring guitar? Where will they go to find the freedom to be themselves, to let it all hang out? And where will they go to see and hear some of the incredible musicality and creativity our city has to offer?

This wasn't on the menu at my local hipster cafe, last time I checked.

But there's also the next crop of music fans to think about. The disappearance of the Boot would be a tragedy for me, sure, but what about my kids? What about a whole generation who will never get to experience the magic of this place firsthand?

What about aspiring musicians who may never be able to advance their careers, because they have nowhere that will allow them to perform and demonstrate their potential? How many future Trombone Jacksons could remain undiscovered?

As an ageing rocker, I've seen friends and colleagues change over the years: from watching gentrification in our suburbs with disgust, to leading the charge for gentrification themselves.

We had all the benefits of letting loose at The Salty Boot, but now that we're older, more delicate, our generation wants to shut it down.

Because it's too loud. Too loud!

I don't know about you, but when I was a youngster we turned it up to eleven. We drank and screamed and danced all night long, we made art and rock-and-roll – but let these kids do the same?

Absolutely not.

Those of my generation had their fun, and now they're out to ensure that the only thing approaching expression and creativity our children can appreciate is latte art.

Well, folks, I for one am not going to let them pull the plug on this place.

I'm not prepared to say goodbye just yet – and I don't think you are either.

Show your support. Sign the petition to keep our Salty Boot dark, dingy and dirty – and as loud (and proud) as it wants to be. Thank you.

Tips

- Note how the layout of the text reflects the speaker's delivery: he uses strong declamatory sentences and frequent pauses in order to allow his points to be easily absorbed by listeners.
- He also uses frequent rhetorical questions that encourage the listener to reflect on all that might be lost with the closure of The Salty Boot. The way in which these form a list of potential losses makes the situation seem grave and implies that much more is at stake than just a place to hear live music. These questions also serve to lend his speech gravitas and importance, inclining his audience to pay attention. Moreover, this repetitious strategy has associations with poetry and music, a reminder to the audience of the value of live performance.
- Examine the speaker's tone and the ways in which he uses humour and emotional appeals to stir both nostalgia and a sense of outrage in his audience.
- The speaker's own personality and experiences are a key element of his argument. Look for the points at which he refers to himself and consider the persona he projects and how this might incline the audience to respond to his point of view.
- Examine the visual style of the flyer and the way in which the visual tone supports the speaker's tone. Take into account the fact that the flyer's creator, like D'Angelo, is a long-time supporter of the venue, and consider how their joint purpose and shared approach is likely to strengthen their argument in the minds of the audience.

Scenario 9: Golf course development

Instructions

- In this section, you are required to analyse the use of argument(s) and language to persuade an intended audience to share the point of view expressed in an unseen persuasive text.
- Read the background information on this page and the material on the following pages, and write an analytical response to the task below.
- For the purposes of this task, the term 'language' refers to written and spoken language, and 'visuals' refers to images and graphics.
- This section is worth one-third of the total marks for the examination.

Task

Write an analysis of the ways in which argument(s), written and spoken language, and visuals are used in the material on the following pages to try to persuade the intended audience to share the point of view presented.

Background information

A new golf course development has been proposed for the old Showgrounds area in Westhaven. The local council is yet to approve the proposal. One of the landscape architects working on the project, Alejandra Ortega, addressed a community gathering to inform them about the development plans. The following is a transcript of her speech, along with two of the projected images from the presentation.

Good evening, my fellow community members, and thank you for joining me here tonight to discuss this amazing opportunity. I'm going to tell you a little bit more about our plans, and invite your feedback on ways that we can make this development even more exciting and inclusive. For those of you who don't know me, I'm Alejandra Ortega, and I am the director of Ortega Landscape Design, but far more importantly I'm a local Westhaven girl through and through. I grew up here – just round the corner on Regan Street, actually – and I love this town as much as you all clearly do. Which is why, when Goodgreens Developers approached my firm to design their new golf course, I could not say yes quickly enough.

Figures from the ausgolf website show that Australia has more golf clubs per capita than almost any other country. Did you know that, in 2020, golf participation in Australia showed the highest increase of any organised sport? An official Sport Australia survey showed that 250 000 more Australians played golf than in the previous year. Despite COVID – or perhaps even because of it – more and more Australians are beginning to enjoy the benefits of the sport. Seeking a gentle form of aerobic exercise? Golf! Looking for a like-minded community to share physical and social activity with? Golf! Hoping to improve your hand-eye coordination and develop your ability to hit a really small white ball with a really thin stick into a tiny hole a really long way away? Golf, golf, golf!

Now, I know that many of you are concerned about the proposed location for the new course, at the old Westhaven Showgrounds. Currently, as you probably all know, the grounds are managed by the council and, in addition to being freely accessible to the public, can be booked for community activities such as parties, school events and weddings. However, our research, with the support of the council, shows that public bookings for the area have declined by over 40% in the last four years. This indicates that the community is not making use of the facilities. While I know some people still come to the local parkrun on the oval, take their kids to the playground and occasionally use the barbecue areas, this is not enough to justify leaving the area undeveloped.

The Showgrounds is an underutilised space that the council cannot afford to maintain properly, and it is becoming tragically run down. The rusting grandstand, dilapidated fencing and old toilet block urgently need upgrading as well as ongoing maintenance, which will require new and sustainable revenue streams. If you have a look at the photo on the screen behind me, you will see exactly what I mean.

We all want to have pride in our local environment, and building a golf course at the Showgrounds will rejuvenate this space not only for tourists but also for our own local residents. Now, have a look at this next slide. This is what our new space could look like – isn't that a terrific improvement?!

The partnership between Goodgreens Developers and Ortega Landscape Design has so much to offer our community. As private developers, we have a significant budget at our disposal, meaning that we can bring the Showgrounds to life in a way that has not been seen since the days when the site hosted the bustling, exciting Westhaven Shows many decades ago. The proposed Greenhaven Golf Club will value-add to our community. It will give residents the opportunity to nurture or begin a passion for golf without having to travel away from Westhaven. It will revitalise an area that is not appreciated currently. And, perhaps most significantly, it will bring much-needed tourist dollars. We have a beautiful and vibrant town, and now is the time to showcase it to travellers.

Many of you fear losing your community space. But let me assure you that the project is not designed to alienate anyone. The development plan – which is here for you to view tonight – includes a club restaurant open to the public, a special mini-golf course dedicated to introducing children to the sport, and a purpose-built public running track that will take advantage of the new greenscape the club will generate. Far from losing a space, you will find a whole new world open to you at Greenhaven, whether you are a dedicated golfer or a health-conscious Westhaven resident seeking fresh air and exercise in beautiful, well-kept parklands.

Please feel free to come up and chat with me shortly about any questions or concerns you may have. We expect this development proposal to be approved in the next few months, and we want to be sure we have had the input of all our most valued stakeholders, both financial and personal – and that means you.

Thanks for your time, and I look forward to seeing you on the greens!

Tips

- » Be aware of the speaker's vested interest in the golf course development, which she reveals at the outset of her speech ('I am the director of Ortega Landscape Design'). In declaring this upfront she aims to present herself as open and honest in order to establish trust in her audience; while this position obviously suggests a potential bias in her viewpoint, it also indicates a level of knowledge and expertise about the site and proposed development.
- » Note, however, the way in which she moves quickly on from this point to emphasise her connection to the local area ('but far more importantly I'm a local Westhaven girl through and through'), thus conveying the impression that her opinion on the development derives from her knowledge and love of the place in which she grew up, rather than any business interest in the golf course.
- » Ortega creates an extended appeal to civic pride in her speech, reminding her audience that they live in a 'beautiful and vibrant town' and invoking shame at the current state of the Showgrounds site through the description of it as 'run down', supported by the photograph showing the dingy and damaged stands. The contrasting second image depicts the sunlit proposed golf course; showing children using the facilities associates the golf course with the bright future Ortega describes.
- » Note, too, the way in which Ortega encourages her audience to view themselves not only as 'our most valued stakeholders' but as important decision-makers. This is true of the council members who will vote on the proposed golf course, but is not the case for most of the people she addresses. Nevertheless, this flattery is intended to make her listeners feel valued and important, and thus to wish to side with the person who is evoking these positive feelings.

Scenario 10: Fast fashion

Instructions

- In this section, you are required to analyse the use of argument(s) and language to persuade an intended audience to share the point of view expressed in an unseen persuasive text.
- Read the background information on this page and the material on the following pages, and write an analytical response to the task below.
- For the purposes of this task, the term 'language' refers to written and spoken language, and 'visuals' refers to images and graphics.
- This section is worth one-third of the total marks for the examination.

Task

Write an analysis of the ways in which argument(s), written and spoken language, and visuals are used in the material on the following pages to try to persuade the intended audience to share the point of view presented.

Background information

Alessandra DuBois, owner of the second-hand clothing store Alessandra's Thrifty Chic Store, has written a lengthy post on a blog linked with her store's website. She has shared the post with followers of her store on different social media platforms.

Fast fashion? Let's slow it down

By Alessandra DuBois

Does the person in this cartoon look familiar? Someone who buys on-trend outfits and must-have accessories, without taking the time to consider the ramifications of their shopping habits – in other words, a proponent of fast fashion. If this sounds like someone you know, send them this post immediately. **This is their intervention**.

For those of you unfamiliar with the term, 'fast fashion' refers to trendy, inexpensive clothing inspired by catwalks and/or celebrity trends and made available at rapid speed to cater to the demands of consumers. While this may sound like a good thing to those on a budget who like to keep up with trends, it grossly ignores a toxic culture that harms the environment and exploits workers.

Currently, the fashion industry churns out 80 billion garments a year – that's 400% more than 20 years ago! And according to clothes waste charity TRAID, the average garment is only worn ten times before it is thrown away. The environmental impact of endlessly producing new clothes in this way is colossal.

Every year the fashion sector requires 93 billion cubic metres of water, and wastewater from the factories producing the clothes gets dumped directly into rivers. This toxic water, containing substances such as lead, mercury and arsenic, threatens both wildlife and humans. Furthermore, fast fashion leads to high levels of plastic pollution. Over 60% of clothes are manufactured using petrochemicals, and these fabrics are not biodegradable in nature. Also, according to the Ellen MacArthur Foundation, clothes release half a million tonnes of microfibres into the ocean every year, equivalent to more than 50 billion plastic bottles.

If that wasn't enough to scare you, the industry also has a heavy carbon footprint. *The Ethical Consumer* has suggested that the production of clothes could amount to 26% of our total carbon footprint in less than 30 years if these trends in fast fashion continue on their upward trajectory.

This highlights the urgency of the issue – it's so important that it affects the very future of our planet. You may think that something as simple as the clothes you wear on your back is insignificant – that 'this stuff … has nothing to do with you', to quote everyone's favourite fashion horror flick, *The Devil Wears Prada* – but the decisions you make today about how and where you purchase your clothes will have significant consequences for us all.

And let's not forget the human element in all of this: that is, the people who make the clothes with their own two hands, working unbearably long hours for terribly low pay (below the living wage) under extremely hazardous working conditions. Many of these workers are found in countries such as Bangladesh, China and India, where sweatshops and child labour are rife.

Given all this, how can anyone consciously continue to support fast fashion? Especially when there's such a simple fix for this issue.

As I'm sure many of you are aware, I opened Alessandra's Thrifty Chic Store two years ago. Today, it is Brunswick's premier second hand clothing business and a prime alternative to the large outlets that promote fast fashion.

Our products are all sustainably sourced and carefully selected to ensure they're made from durable materials – this means you'll get hundreds if not thousands of uses out of them before they need to be disposed of.

By encouraging our patrons to donate clothing rather than simply throwing it out, we can stop the vicious cycle of wastage, and offer those on a budget the chance to purchase stylish outfits without contributing their hard-earned dollars to an abusive system.

Second-hand clothes stores aren't the only way you can help challenge the spread of fast fashion, though. It's important to note that not every fashion brand is considered fast fashion, and that an increasing number of brands are conscious of community and environmental issues. These are the ones who choose to use natural materials, eco-friendly manufacturing and fair labour. Purchasing garments that are made from recyclable or environmentally friendly materials, from companies such as these, will have a lower negative impact on our waterways, air and soil once you have finished using them.

Whether it's shopping at a thrift store or carefully selecting garments that you can wear for years and years, this trend of 'slow fashion' is what we need to see more of. If everyone who sees this post went to their closet right now and gathered every item of clothing they were planning to dispose of and donated them to a thrift store, we would have collectively made a sizeable difference in bringing fast fashion to a screeching halt. So, get out there and spread the message: the era of fast fashion is dead.

Tips

» The writer opens with a question to the reader, with the aim of immediately capturing their attention. The directness of this approach is likely to be well received by her target audience of readers who are probably familiar with her social media profile and already interested in fashion. The description of the female figure who appears in the image at the start of the blog post aims to retain this attention through its familiarity and relatability.

» DuBois instructs readers to 'send ... this post immediately' to anyone they believe resembles the person described in her opening paragraph. Keep in mind the multiple purposes this fulfils. It continues the direct address and intimate tone established from the outset, which draws on the existing relationship between the writer and many of her readers to deepen rapport. It implies a likelihood that her readers will recognise this type of person in their own lives, suggesting the problem of fast fashion is significant. It also further promotes the writer's own social media presence and business under the guise of an 'intervention', a word usually used to describe the loving involvement of family and friends in an addict's treatment.

» Consider the two types of argument DuBois presents for rejecting fast fashion: that it is unethical, and that not buying fast fashion is easy and beneficial for consumers, as implied with phrases such as 'simple fix' and 'you'll get hundreds if not thousands of uses out of them'. In this way she positions readers to think that shopping ethically is good for the environment, for others and for themselves.

Scenario 11: Sunflower plantations

Instructions

- In this section, you are required to analyse the use of argument(s) and language to persuade an intended audience to share the point of view expressed in an unseen persuasive text.
- Read the background information on this page and the material on the following pages, and write an analytical response to the task below.
- For the purposes of this task, the term 'language' refers to written and spoken language, and 'visuals' refers to images and graphics.
- This section is worth one-third of the total marks for the examination.

Task

Write an analysis of the ways in which argument(s), written and spoken language, and visuals are used in the material on the following pages to try to persuade the intended audience to share the point of view presented.

Background information

The small town of Sunnyside is well known for its sunflower plantations, a major contributor to the town's economy. Recently, Sunnyside has been inundated with tourists visiting the fields and taking photos. The number of visitors has caused stress to the crops and is upsetting farmers. One farmer, Harvey Sunshine, called an emergency council meeting to address the problem. The following is a transcript of the speech he delivered, with a photograph that accompanied the speech.

Ladies and gentleman of our beloved community: for those who haven't had the great displeasure, my name is Harvey Sunshine, long-time local of Sunnyside and resident curmudgeon.

Most of you have come to know me as the man with a constant axe to grind, and while that reputation is partly warranted, it's not something I take lightly: every now and then, axes need grinding and we must speak our mind, loudly and clearly.

I've called this meeting today to talk about an issue of increasing concern for our community.

For the past two summers, I, like many of my fellow farmers, have been dealing with a huge increase in the number of tourists visiting my sunflower fields.

Tourists have always been a presence at Sunnyside. We live in a beautiful part of the world, after all, and the sunflowers in full bloom are something truly special to behold.

But the sheer number arriving in the summer months is causing havoc across the region.

People tell me it's a 'social media' problem, and that what these folks are after is a photo or two to share on the internet.

But the damage they're willing to cause in the service of that one perfect shot is, frankly, disturbing.

They arrive in hordes – sometimes hundreds a day – parking along the single road that runs by my property, clogging up the traffic.

They come armed to the teeth with 'selfie sticks' and snacks.

Some of them – the decent ones – enter through my front gate and ask permission to take a photo, but the rest are scaling my fence, or cutting the wires.

I've seen people trample hundreds of dollars underfoot. I've seen others snap the heads off my plants and take them home. You'll see in the photo I've put up on the wall behind me the kinds of damage I'm witnessing daily in the summer.

Harvey Sunshine inspects his sunflowers for damage.

And it's not just the plants that are suffering. My two dogs, Banjo and Lucky, are in a constant state of anxiety and hypervigilance due to the constant intrusions. My cat, Millicent, is scared to step foot outside most days, for fear of being hounded for pats and pictures by perfect strangers. And long gone are the days when I could let the grandkids wander freely among the fields – no chance of that when I've no idea who they might encounter in a place they ought to be able to have free and private enjoyment of.

That word – 'private' – is a key one. Call me old-fashioned but I think it's something we can still, even in this publicity-obsessed age, reasonably expect in our own homes and backyards.

And yet I've spent days clearing litter from my property and hours arguing with the belligerents who think they have a right to wander around my farm without a care in the world.

'Well, what's to be done?' you ask.

As far as the council is concerned, there's nothing we can do. 'Put up and shut up until the season is over,' they tell us.

Absolute cowardice!

We need urgent and concerted action if sunflowers are to have any kind of future here in our community.

My solution? Simple. Or, at least, simple economics. If these people want to take photos of the crops then we should let them – but at a price. I'm suggesting we farmers charge a fee to the tourists who enter our property and take photos of the flowers.

This is, after all, a very fragile plant, and one that only blooms during a small window of time in the year.

Charging these people is a way to help our farmers get through the non-productive season with a little extra to invest when the next crop comes around.

It's not just the farmers who would benefit, either. Think of what a boon a little extra money would be to our community, to our local businesses.

And then there are the opportunities to explore new ventures. Coffee carts outside every farm. Local markets selling fresh produce from around the region. The potential is limitless.

I know of a number of towns in other regions doing the same thing. Dandyville is already reaping the benefits of asking tourists to pay to see their flower plantations, and we can't let them get ahead of us.

Whether you can believe it or not, people are willing to pay to take photos of our sunflowers, and we have a choice: let them do so, or let our farmers wear the bill for leaving the situation as it is. And take it from me, we farmers won't – can't – afford to wear these costs indefinitely. I don't want to shut up shop or be forced out of the home I love. But the situation has reached a crisis point.

So I'm calling on all of you to get behind our farmers and get behind our community. Support my motion for implementing a town-wide price of admission to our sunflower fields. Support our local businesses. Support the future of Sunnyside!

Tips

- Think about why Sunshine might begin by describing himself as a 'curmudgeon' with an 'axe to grind', an unflattering characterisation. What is the likely impact of this on an audience of mostly local people and how might it prepare them to receive his opinion?
- Consider why Sunshine might have chosen to place a photo of himself in the sunflower fields behind him as he speaks. Together with his humorous description of himself, it works to suggest a gruff but good-hearted persona, whose perspective on the issue can be relied upon to be sincere. The warm light of the sunshine in the image, as well as Sunshine's gentle inspection of the flowers, suggests his genuine care for them and supports his argument for protecting them.
- Although he describes in some detail the impact of visitors on his sunflower plantation, Sunshine also notes the impact on his animals, grandchildren, other farmers and the community generally, thus suggesting that he is as concerned for others as he is for himself and his financial interests. This impression of compassion is likely to resonate with an audience consisting of people who probably have their own land, families and animals that they want to protect.
- Look at the language Sunshine uses to describe the visitors – for example, words such as 'hordes', 'clogging', 'belligerents', 'strangers' – and reflect on the overall impression he builds up of these tourists. Contrast this with the image he presents of vulnerable plants and farmers and consider how this contributes to the 'us and them' dynamic he aims to promote, with the heedless visitors threatening the innocent residents of Sunnyside.

Scenario 12: Video games in the English classroom

Instructions

- In this section, you are required to analyse the use of argument(s) and language to persuade an intended audience to share the point of view expressed in an unseen persuasive text.
- Read the background information on this page and the material on the following pages, and write an analytical response to the task below.
- For the purposes of this task, the term 'language' refers to written and spoken language, and 'visuals' refers to images and graphics.
- This section is worth one-third of the total marks for the examination.

Task

Write an analysis of the ways in which argument(s), written and spoken language, and visuals are used in the material on the following pages to try to persuade the intended audience to share the point of view presented.

Background information

Margaret Lee has been invited to participate in a state conference for English teachers. An experienced English teacher, she has spent the past few years developing resources to help teachers incorporate video games into their English courses. The following is a transcript of the presentation she made at the start of her workshop. Two images were projected on a screen while she was speaking, each shown at different points during her speech as indicated by their placement in the transcript.

Good afternoon to my fellow English teachers. Thank you for welcoming me to speak to you today. I'm here to present a new opportunity for your students, one that will offer them an exciting new way to learn, to analyse and to study English.

I'm talking, of course, about video games.

Now, I understand that some of you have been teaching English for decades, and might never have thought of video games as a learning tool. You might even believe that video games lead to aggression and laziness. But these past few years I've been working with schools to incorporate video games into their English courses with great success.

So I ask you to forget about the violent, repetitive games you might have encountered before, and allow me to introduce you to a new world of English texts, the modern universe of video games.

Long gone are the days of punching sticky buttons in an arcade, pointlessly trying to beat your high score. Long gone are the days of zoning out in front of the TV in a darkened room, spending hours trying to master an impossible level.

The games I'm talking about are infinitely more sophisticated. In fact, they are closer to works of art than to actual games. They include engaging storylines, stunning animation and moving music scores, much like some of the films that we're already so used to analysing in English classrooms.

Furthermore, video games have several advantages over other texts.

Most video games offer an open world for the player to explore, meaning they make their own choices as they play. These choices then have consequences later in the game, so the concept of narrative structure is embedded into the act of playing. Additionally, players are able to take on new identities as they play, allowing them to empathise with characters who are very different from themselves.

Cognitive scientists have carried out several studies that suggest playing video games can improve decision-making skills and increase coordination, things that can't be developed while merely reading a novel.

And that's just the start of it.

Some video games on the market present historically accurate worlds, which can give students an advantage as they learn about historical context. Side quests and background characters can provide insight into the conventions of a genre and how society functions within that world. From exploring a precise replica of an ancient Italian city to helping a woman with a lame horse in the Wild West, playing these games can help students retain clear visual memories of the text they're studying, much more easily than if they were reading words printed on a page.

When I was still teaching English myself – I won't lie to you – I hated the idea of replacing even one of the texts on my list with a video game. I couldn't imagine removing any novel, play or group of poems. For some of my students, those books were likely to be the only classics they would ever have the opportunity to study. And how many of us would choose to play a game with killer robots when we could curl up with a book by our favourite author?

Then I considered my students.

I considered what makes them excited to learn.

I considered the world outside my classroom.

I considered the challenges that some of my students face with English.

And I knew I needed to put aside my own preferences in order to help them. For some, the English class is the worst part of their day. We forget how difficult it can be to relate to characters and situations from hundreds of years ago. For some, the task of finishing a class novel can be arduous, and it can even discourage struggling students from reading outside of class.

Video games give them a chance to really engage with a text in a more relaxed and fun way, while still learning how to analyse and interpret. Once they learn those tools, who's to say those students won't feel a bit more confident about picking up that novel again?

Of course, I understand that some of you are feeling reluctant to take this big step in your classrooms. After all, we're English teachers! We wouldn't be here if we didn't love the written word. But we can't deny that video games are becoming more and more advanced.

It would be a shame to leave these rich texts unexplored when we have them right at our fingertips.

Tips

- Notice the way in which Lee repeatedly references her own experiences as a teacher to establish her credentials with her audience of fellow teachers. This is aimed at helping them feel that she understands the challenges of the classroom as well as their potential reluctance to use video games as texts, a reluctance she admits to having once shared. In this way she encourages them to share her journey from scepticism to appreciation.
- This appeal to her audience as fellow professional educators is extended through her references to pedagogical terminology associated with English teaching, such as 'genre', 'narrative structure' and 'rich texts'. The use of this familiar language is intended to reassure teachers that Lee is experienced and knowledgeable, and that therefore her conclusions are likely to be reliable.
- Reflecting the fact that this is a spoken text, several sentences are set as standalone paragraphs, around which Lee would allow brief pauses. This technique highlights key points and allows the audience time to absorb them.
- The repeated 'I considered' standalone statements serve multiple functions: they remind the listener that Lee's position has been arrived at after careful contemplation; they encourage listeners to themselves take time to consider new perspectives on video games, just as Lee has; they emphasise that it is students' needs that should be prioritised in the context of this debate; and they contribute to an oratorical mood that lends Lee's claims gravity and a sense of significance.

Scenario 13: Keeping cats indoors

Instructions

- In this section, you are required to analyse the use of argument(s) and language to persuade an intended audience to share the point of view expressed in an unseen persuasive text.
- Read the background information on this page and the material on the following pages, and write an analytical response to the task below.
- For the purposes of this task, the term 'language' refers to written and spoken language, and 'visuals' refers to images and graphics.
- This section is worth one-third of the total marks for the examination.

Task

Write an analysis of the ways in which argument(s), written and spoken language, and visuals are used in the material on the following pages to try to persuade the intended audience to share the point of view presented.

Background information

The following article, by a team of professors and academics about the danger outdoor cats can pose to local wildlife, was first published on *The Conversation*.

One cat, one year, 110 native animals: lock up your pet, it's a killing machine

By Jaana Dielenberg, Brett Murphy, Chris Dickman, John Woinarski, Leigh-Ann Woolley, Mike Calver and Sarah Legge

We know feral cats are an enormous problem for wildlife – across Australia, feral cats collectively kill more than three billion animals per year. Cats have played a leading role in most of Australia's 34 mammal extinctions since 1788, and are a big reason populations of at least 123 other threatened native species are dropping.

But pet cats are wreaking havoc too. Our analysis compiles the results of 66 different studies to gauge the impact of Australia's pet cat population on the country's wildlife.

The results are staggering. On average, each roaming pet cat kills 186 reptiles, birds and mammals per year, most of them native to Australia. Collectively, that's 4,440 to 8,100 animals per square kilometre per year for the area inhabited by pet cats.

If you own a cat and want to protect wildlife, you should keep it inside. In Australia, 1.1 million pet cats are contained 24 hours a day by responsible pet owners. The remaining 2.7 million pet cats – 71% of all pet cats – are able to roam and hunt. What's more, your pet cat could be getting out without you knowing. A radio tracking study in Adelaide found that of the 177 cats whom owners believed were inside at night, 69 cats (39%) were sneaking out for nocturnal adventures.

Surely not my cat

Just over one-quarter of Australian households (27%) have pet cats, and about half of cat-owning households have two or more cats. Many owners believe their animals don't hunt because they never come across evidence of killed animals.

But studies that used cat video tracking collars or scat analysis (checking what's in the cat's poo) have established many pet cats kill animals without bringing them home. On average, pet cats bring home only 15% of their prey.

Collectively, roaming pet cats kill 390 million animals per year in Australia.

This huge number may lead some pet owners to think their own cat's contribution wouldn't make much difference. However, we found even single pet cats have driven declines and complete losses of populations of some native animal species in their area. Documented cases have included: a feather-tailed glider population in south-eastern NSW; a skink population in a Perth suburb; and an olive legless lizard population in Canberra.

Urban cats

On average, an individual feral cat in the bush kills 748 reptiles, birds and mammals a year – four times the toll of a hunting pet cat. But feral cats and pet cats roam over very different areas. Pet cats are confined to cities and towns, where you'll find 40 to 70 roaming cats per square kilometre. In the bush there's only one feral cat for every three to four square kilometres. So while each pet cat kills fewer animals than a feral cat, their high urban density means the toll is still very high. Per square kilometre per year, pet cats kill 30–50 times more animals than feral cats in the bush.

Most of us want to see native wildlife around towns and cities. But such a vision is being compromised by this extraordinary level of predation, especially as the human population grows and our cities expand.

Pet cats living near areas with nature also hunt more, reducing the value of places that should be safe havens for wildlife. The 186 animals each pet cat kills per year on average is made up of 110 native animals (40 reptiles, 38 birds and 32 mammals). For example, the critically endangered western ringtail possum is found in suburban areas of Mandurah, Bunbury, Busselton and Albany. The possum did not move into these areas – rather, we moved into their habitat.

What can pet owners do?

Keeping your cat securely contained 24 hours a day is the only way to prevent it from killing wildlife.

It's a myth that a good diet or feeding a cat more meat will prevent hunting: even cats that aren't hungry will hunt. Various devices, such as bells on collars, are commercially marketed with the promise of preventing hunting. While some of these items may reduce the rate of successful kills, they don't prevent hunting altogether.

And they don't prevent cats from disturbing wildlife. When cats prowl and hunt in an area, wildlife have to spend more time hiding or escaping. This reduces the time spent feeding themselves or their young, or resting. In Mandurah, WA, the disturbance and hunting of just one pet cat and one stray cat caused the total breeding failure of a colony of more than 100 pairs of fairy terns.

Benefits of a life indoors

Keeping cats indoors protects pet cats from injury, avoids nuisance behaviour and prevents unwanted breeding. Cats allowed outside often get into fights with other cats, even when they're not the fighting type (they can be attacked by other cats).

Roaming cats are also very prone to getting hit by vehicles. According to the Humane Society of the United States, indoor cats live up to four times longer than those allowed to roam freely.

Indoor cats have lower rates of cat-borne diseases, some of which can infect humans. For example, in humans the cat-borne disease toxoplasmosis can cause illness, miscarriages and birth defects.

But Australia is in a very good position to make change. Compared to many other countries, the Australian public are more aware of how cats threaten native wildlife and more supportive of actions to reduce those impacts.

It won't be easy. But since more than one million pet cats are already being contained, reducing the impacts from pet cats is clearly possible if we take responsibility for them.

Tips

- The image at the beginning of the piece neatly encapsulates the issue from the outset, vividly supporting the writers' argument about cats' potential for destruction. The fact that the cat depicted is an average-sized common domestic cat encourages readers to recognise that their own pets could be part of the problem, while the dead or injured bird is a stark reminder of the damage they can do to smaller, innocent creatures. The cat also looms over the bird, taking up most of the image's frame, highlighting the danger it presents to local wildlife.
- This text relies heavily on facts and statistics, which is linked to its place of publication – on the website of *The Conversation*, which publishes pieces by journalists and academics based on rigorous research. This context of publication means that the reader expects a certain level of fact-checking and logical rigour, thus inclining them to place more trust in the writers' conclusions.
- This reliance on research is supported by the writers' straightforward and definite tone. They make many declarative statements – for example, 'we know feral cats are an enormous problem for wildlife' and 'if you own a cat and want to protect wildlife, you should keep it inside'. Such statements leave little room for disagreement, conveying the impression that the writers are presenting indisputable facts and positioning the reader to accept their views as authoritative.
- Understanding that many of their readers will be cat-owners themselves, the writers are careful to emphasise the benefits of keeping cats indoors in terms of cat welfare. Ending with this point of argument aims to leave the reader with a positive impression of the practice of keeping cats inside, rather than a sense that the animals will be disadvantaged by an indoors existence.

Scenario 14: Tax on red meat

Instructions

- In this section, you are required to analyse the use of argument(s) and language to persuade an intended audience to share the point of view expressed in an unseen persuasive text.
- Read the background information on this page and the material on the following pages, and write an analytical response to the task below.
- For the purposes of this task, the term 'language' refers to written and spoken language, and 'visuals' refers to images and graphics.
- This section is worth one-third of the total marks for the examination.

Task

Write an analysis of the ways in which argument(s), written and spoken language, and visuals are used in the material on the following pages to try to persuade the intended audience to share the point of view presented.

Background information

Parminder Preciosa is a columnist for a local newspaper. Her opinion piece calling for a tax on red meat appears on the following pages.

Taxing the T-bone: it's time to give red meat the chop

By Parminder Preciosa

Allow me to set the scene.

It's lunchtime at your favourite al fresco restaurant and you've just placed your order. One glass of wine and the special of the day, your favourite: bangers and mash.

The food arrives promptly and the waiter departs with a top-up of your glass and a kindly 'bon appétit'.

The moment you've been waiting for is here, but just as you ready yourself to take that first bite – fork in hand, napkin in collar, salivating at the expectation – you smell it.

Smoke.

Cigarette smoke, specifically.

Wafting over to your table. Stinging your eyes. Clinging to the insides of your nostrils.

The culprit is well beyond the no-smoking area (you've checked), but it doesn't matter – the odour is overpowering. Your potatoes with thyme have taken on the taste of a menthol slim; your glass of red wine resembles a puddle on a dirty bitumen road.

It's disgusting, you think to yourself. Another selfish durry-muncher, poisoning themselves – and those in the wider radius – with their dirty vice, gobbling up your healthcare tax dollars and making life uncomfortable for everyone else.

You're mad. You're furious. You're going to say something! And, to be honest, not many people would blame you.

Because, there's no doubt, it's easy to get angry about smoking in the twenty-first century.

The latest statistics suggest that 10.6 per cent of Australia's adults smoke, and the government is making sure those who can't quit know all about the cost of their habit, both to our society and to themselves.

Cigarettes are now taxed to high heaven, and the packages they come in are covered in images of the gruesome medical conditions that can befall even the most casual puffer.

But while you might be hyper-aware of the dangers of smoking, there's another killer in this picture, and it's hiding in plain sight. Yep, right there, next to your mash.

I'm talking about the bangers. Sausages. Red meat: delicious, maybe, but just as much of a threat to your health as that packet of cigs.

The World Health Organization (WHO) now classifies red meat as a carcinogen, with the consumption of processed varieties such as sausages, ham and corned beef showing an elevated risk to humans.

According to *BMJ Global Health Journal*, if people were to replace their red meat with small fish such as sardines, herring and anchovies, up to 750 000 premature deaths from non-communicable diseases such as stroke or colon cancer could be prevented by 2050, especially in low- and middle-income countries. A study published in *Proceedings of the National Academy of Sciences* found that up to 16 000 deaths in the United States can be attributed to air pollution caused by food production, and 80 per cent of these are the result of animal-related food production, including meat production.

But mention any of these statistics to your average punter, and you're sure to draw looks of incredulity.

Pepperoni pizza, bacon and eggs – fatal? But they're so delicious!

Sorry, people, but that's pretty much what they said about cigarettes once upon a time.

It wasn't easy to change the way we as a society think about smoking, and it's not going to be easy to change the way we think about red meat, either.

But just because something is difficult in the beginning, that doesn't mean it isn't worth doing.

It's time to treat meat the way we treat other threats to human health, and the first step should be taxing consumption.

Taxes such as the ones we have on cigarettes would address the enormous strain on our health budgets associated with eating red meat.

Taxes would also have positive knock-on effects that go beyond the economic, like encouraging people to make healthier choices.

But even if the health argument won't convince you, there are myriad other reasons for bringing in a meat tax.

One issue worth considering is how red meat production is affecting the planet.

Livestock farming is posing a catastrophic risk to our ecosystem, from the large amounts of greenhouse gases animals produce and the water needed to sustain them (500 grams of beef is estimated to require some 7000 litres of water), to the swathes of carbon-absorbing forests being cleared to accommodate more farms. And with demand for red meat growing globally, the problem is only going to get worse.

Animal rights groups have also pointed to the sometimes appalling ways we treat the animals we eat, including the unethical practices adopted to raise and slaughter millions of cows and pigs each year. (Australia kills an astonishing 170 000 cattle alone each week.)

The case, then – to my mind, at least – is clear. And in some ways it's more persuasive than the arguments for taxing cigarettes.

Red meat has costs: economically, ethically and in terms of our health. And while it's nobody's right to dictate what people can and can't do, it's reasonable that individuals should pay for those activities that place a burden on all of us, be it smoking that cigarette or tucking into a T-bone.

Tips

» Preciosa opens with an extended description of a diner being disturbed by cigarette smoke. The details she includes to paint the picture – such as the meal ordered and the waiter's words – together with the distinctive use of the second-person 'you', invite readers to place themselves in this situation and encourage them to feel the same disgust and upset provoked by the fictional smoker. This suggests to readers that the dislike of cigarette smoke is universal, thus preparing them for her main argument that they should feel similarly about meat.

» Drawing a comparison between the familiar and widely accepted opinion that cigarette smoking is bad for one's health, and the argument that meat consumption is harmful, prepares the reader to accept that meat poses similar dangers. Through this comparison, Preciosa associates the harm caused by cigarettes with that caused by meat, creating a connection in readers' minds that is likely to position them to want to stop eating meat or at least to reduce their meat consumption.

» In comparing meat to cigarettes, the writer aims to evoke both fear and disgust in the reader, a tactic she continues throughout her piece. The image supports this strategy by presenting a slab of raw meat on a plate, an unappetising sight that is likely to arouse the viewer's sense of disgust. The question mark shape alludes to the dilemma of whether or not to eat red and processed meat, encouraging viewers to reflect on their choices in light of the information shared by Preciosa.

» Note that the main argument Preciosa presents is that red and processed meats are bad for people's health. She devotes the most space to this argument, presenting various forms of evidence. However, she also presents additional supporting reasons, referring to the environmental and animal welfare benefits of a meat tax. It is worth spending more time in your analysis on the way in which Preciosa unpacks and supports her primary reason than on the supplementary reasons she offers.

Scenario 15: Coffee pods

Instructions

- In this section, you are required to analyse the use of argument(s) and language to persuade an intended audience to share the point of view expressed in an unseen persuasive text.
- Read the background information on this page and the material on the following pages, and write an analytical response to the task below.
- For the purposes of this task, the term 'language' refers to written and spoken language, and 'visuals' refers to images and graphics.
- This section is worth one-third of the total marks for the examination.

Task

Write an analysis of the ways in which argument(s), written and spoken language, and visuals are used in the material on the following pages to try to persuade the intended audience to share the point of view presented.

Background information

The following opinion piece appeared on *The Conversation* website, which claims to provide 'an independent source of news and views, sourced from the academic and research community and delivered direct to the public'.

What our love affair with coffee pods reveals about our values

By John Rice and Nigel Martin

Disclosure statement

John Rice is a member of the Australian Labor Party and the National Tertiary Education Union. He drinks skinny flat whites.

Nigel Martin does not work for, consult, own shares in or receive funding from any company or organisation that would benefit from this article, and has disclosed no relevant affiliations beyond their academic appointment.

A quick shot, but then what? While some used coffee pods like these are recycled, many more end up in the bin.

Mornings just aren't the same. Late sleepers, once troubled only by the quiet gurgle of the boiling kettle, are now shaken from their slumber by the guttural sounds of steaming water being forced through aluminium or plastic coffee pods.

The pods are conveniently secreted into the coffee machine's collecting receptacle, so the pangs of guilt from the latte socialists (and others) are only tweaked when the dank pods require emptying – generally well after the coffee has been consumed.

Wooed by no less than Hollywood star George Clooney, Australia is in love with coffee pods. Pods have taken Australian homes and workplaces by storm.

As is the case for other beverages, Australians have shifted to drinking better quality coffee and pods are part of that mix. While pods are one of the most expensive ways to buy packaged coffee, they are also one of the most convenient.

The Swiss coffee pod innovators at Nespresso (a division of the food behemoth Nestlé) have been joined by usurpers including Germany's Aldi and Italy's Cafitally. Proving that patents are easier to take out than protect, Nespresso's share of the world pod market has been in steep decline. This having been said, the industry is in a rapid phase of growth – sales are soaring – and thus few are complaining.

Yet the news is far from all good. Pods are emblematic of a wider problem in our society, where we often say one thing and generally do another. In this case, where many of us like to speak about being 'green' or living sustainably, even while sipping from a cup of coffee produced by an industry that is about as sustainable as an ageing Soviet nuclear power plant.

If, as some predict, pod use doubles over the next five years, a veritable environmental tsunami is in store. In theory, pods are recyclable. But in practice they are rarely recycled, particularly the plastic variety beloved by the budget-conscious.

Instead, they end in landfill: perhaps a poignant sign for garbage archaeologists a thousand years from now of this generation's environmental profligacy.

Independent consumer group Choice reported that Nespresso had sold an estimated 28 billion capsules worldwide in a year – about 28 million kilograms of aluminium, much of which may be sitting in landfill, with recycling figures not made public.

New Zealand's Ethical Coffee Company has created a vegetable-based biodegradable coffee capsule that is Nespresso-compatible and can be thrown straight into the compost. However, the shelf life of these pods is likely to be far more limited than the most commonly used aluminium or double-wrapped plastic pods.

Environmental problems are not the only vices embodied in pods. The coffee industry has long been wracked by criticism that its sourcing practices, especially in the third world, are rapacious.

The Swiss multinational Nestlé, which first dreamed up the pod phenomenon, is no stranger to such criticism. It runs its own 'sustainability' accreditation program, which it proudly pronounces now exceeds 75% for beans sourced. However, cynics might see the self-accreditation program as essentially self-serving, delivering few benefits or value-adding opportunities to coffee growing communities.

Perhaps most prosaically, critics often argue that pod coffee just isn't any good.

A decent barista generally uses between 10 and 20 grams of ground coffee in a serve, while pods contain barely 5 grams. The decision to make the pods so small was carefully chosen to maximise profits, not taste.

As a result, the coffee produced generally fails blind taste tests – labelled watery, musty and underwhelming by Choice. Hardly the words that the marketers would like to hear.

And yet, the march of the pods continues.

The American satirist HL Mencken famously quipped that 'no one in this world … has ever lost money by underestimating the intelligence of the great masses of the plain people'. In today's world, you could add the word 'laziness' or, more charitably, 'love of convenience' to the list.

Pods, in their own humble way, tell us much about the future intersection of environmentalism and consumerism.

Western consumers are generally supportive of the environment – so long as they don't have to do anything about it. Multinationals everywhere are wise to this, of course, and have created a phenomenon known to cynical greenies and academics as 'greenwashing'. This entails wrapping a product in a veil of environmentally positive haze, regardless of how fundamentally egregious its environmental credentials are.

It all paints a less than rosy picture for the future, in which more businesses help create, rather than solve, environmental problems. How this all plays out remains to be seen. One thing, however, is predictable. For innovators who can blend branding and convenience while ignoring all else, the future seems assured.

Tips

- The writers' overall approach, indicated in the headline, is to frame coffee pod use as part of a broader issue – that people will often act in ways contrary to their expressed values. Readers are encouraged to confront their own hypocrisy or the ways in which they might fall short of their professed environmental ideals, thus positioning them to want to behave differently in order to assuage their sense of guilt.
- Analyse key words that have been carefully chosen for their particular associations. For example, the word 'tsunami', with its connotations of large-sale disaster, death and destruction, aims to evoke alarm in the reader. 'Profligacy' is suggestive of recklessness and irresponsibility, qualities the reader is unlikely to want to be associated with.
- The writers are openly critical not only of coffee pod producers, whom they portray as self-interested profit-seekers, but also of consumers of coffee pods, a group that many readers might fall into. They accuse consumers of valuing 'laziness' and 'love of convenience' over the environment, and their argument is encapsulated in both the headline and the statement that 'Western consumers are generally supportive of the environment – so long as they don't have to do anything about it'. This overt criticism is intended to invoke guilt and shame in readers, if they themselves use coffee pods, and alarm and outrage in non-pod-using readers.
- The bleak conclusion, with its reference to a 'less than rosy' future, conveys the writers' pessimism about the capacity of consumers to change their behaviour, which might evoke in some readers the desire to meet the implicit challenge the writers set: to change their behaviour to match their professed environmental values.

Scenario 16: Children and screen time

Instructions

- In this section, you are required to analyse the use of argument(s) and language to persuade an intended audience to share the point of view expressed in an unseen persuasive text.
- Read the background information on this page and the material on the following pages, and write an analytical response to the task below.
- For the purposes of this task, the term 'language' refers to written and spoken language, and 'visuals' refers to images and graphics.
- This section is worth one-third of the total marks for the examination.

Task

Write an analysis of the ways in which argument(s), written and spoken language, and visuals are used in the material on the following pages to try to persuade the intended audience to share the point of view presented.

Background information

The following letter was written to the Wattletree Primary School community by a parent, Asif Abdul, the father of two students. The letter appeared in the school's weekly newsletter under the heading 'What Steve Jobs taught me about parenting'.

What Steve Jobs taught me about parenting

Dear Wattletree parents,

I've been thinking about something lately, and I'm writing this open letter to encourage you all to do the same. I've been thinking about the amount of time our children spend in front of screens.

Last week, as I was waiting at school to pick up my boys, Joshua and Braiden, I read an interesting article on my phone. It was about how Apple founder Steve Jobs limited his children's screen time.

This got me thinking. If Steve Jobs, technological guru, limited his kids' use of screens, why don't I monitor my children's use?

I did some research and discovered it wasn't only Jobs who felt this way. Several CEOs of tech companies had similar ideas.

I've often used screens to keep my kids quiet. Last week my youngest, Oliver, was with me in a cafe. It had been one of *those* mornings; I couldn't get him to settle down. I asked if he wanted to watch a video. He nodded, raising his eyes hopefully. I propped the phone against the salt shaker and pressed play. He was mesmerised. I finally had a minute to enjoy a coffee.

Later, Oliver watched an hour of television. Then he played on the computer. When his brothers came home, he watched them play video games. After dinner he watched more TV, and in bed we read an ebook on the iPad. Then, while his brothers brushed their teeth, I left the iPad beside him, playing sleep-time music. (It doubles as a night-light.)

Why am I explaining this? Because I've been thinking about the degree to which we're reliant, as parents, on technology: not only for its ability to expose children to new things, or provide answers to curly questions ('Why don't you Google it?' I always tell Braiden), but also as a substitute babysitter. I realised that for me, and I think for many others, communication devices have become an integral part of parenting. When I calculated the amount of time four-year-old Oliver spent in front of a screen, it was almost six hours per day. What effect was that having on his development?

Television, tablets, phones, computers: all these devices are used, often daily, by kids. As I dug further, I found that many reputable figures are concerned by this.

The wonderful book *The Shallows* by Nicholas Carr argues that the internet is changing people's brains in insidious ways we're only beginning to understand. While books encourage a sustained level of concentration and immersion in a story-world, the internet, with its endless links, fosters a shallow, superficial engagement with information – there is always something else to click on. I see this with Braiden, who researches a school project as if running a timed obstacle course – each site only gets a glance before he clicks on something else. He's learning, yes, but what of his learning quality? Is he reflecting on, questioning, synthesising what he reads? Or, with so much at his fingertips, is it encouraging him to skate across the surface, to copy and repeat things, to give little thought to what he is reading?

Many doctors are worried about the effect screen time has on children's brains. Neuroscientist Susan Greenfield thinks neural pathways will change in children who spend hours a day with screens. Professor Gary Small from the US agrees. The American Academy of Pediatrics states that computers should be avoided until a child is two because 'a child's brain develops rapidly during these first years' and 'children learn best by interacting with people, not screens'.

There are also health problems that result from kids being constantly glued to screens. Children are less likely to spend time playing sport or exercising. Since the rise of digital technology, childhood obesity in Australia has increased at a startling rate. (Did you know that, in the decade to 1995, the number of overweight children aged 7–15 almost doubled, and the number of obese children more than tripled?) There's eye strain – on developing eyeballs – and dehydration and sleep problems (exposure to backlit screens at night can affect sleep patterns).

Between computers, tablets, smart phones and television, many Australian children spend hours looking at screens every day.

Cyberbullying and exposure to adult content are also risks. It's estimated that 30 per cent of Aussie children have seen something online that 'upset or bothered them'. As a parent, I try to monitor my kids' internet use, but I can't be watching every second – just as a teacher with a class full of kids can't – to ensure my son doesn't click on a bad link, or Google a 'naughty' word when my back is turned.

Some may ask: if a phone keeps your kid quiet, why worry? Well, like most parents, I want my children to become informed, creative and imaginative adults who contribute to the world in positive, meaningful ways. I have been irresponsible in my quick-fix habits: in seeing screens as a necessity, I have encouraged my children to do so too. Rather than teaching them that devices are a learning tool, I've let my kids use screens to ward off boredom or fatigue or anger. If I'm honest, I've been guilty of the belief that anything involving a screen is good, when in fact overuse might be changing my children's brains – potentially hampering their capacity for sustained critical thought or opening them up to a host of problems later in life. If this sounds like you, I hope you can learn from my mistakes.

Technology has many benefits, but Jobs was onto something. I've implemented a policy in our house: 90 minutes' screen time a day. And if I want Oliver to be quiet, I pull out crayons and ask him to draw, rather than plonk him down in front of a screen. Every night this week we've been reading print books, so he can have dreams sparked by creativity and imagination and wonder, not by blinking lights and flashing figures.

I encourage all parents to think about their children's screen use. As the dictum goes, 'The medium is the message'. The way our children approach the world is being shaped by time spent with screens, and we need to be aware of the responsibilities of that.

Asif Abdul (parent)

Tips

- The headline makes use of the highly recognisable name of Steve Jobs to promote engagement with the article. Jobs was associated with the field of technology, thus the unlikely pairing of his name with the word 'parenting' is aimed at intriguing readers and enticing them to want to find out the connection between the two.
- Notice the way in which Abdul develops a confessional tone, admitting to being 'irresponsible' and to having made 'mistakes'. This helps readers to view him as both relatable and also a figure of sympathy, inclining them to trust that his opinion is both sincere and derived from experience and trial and error.
- This confessional tone is augmented by Abdul's frequent references to his own life and parenting experiences. He introduces his children to readers by name and relates personal information about their moods and habits. This helps to build the impression that he is talking confidentially, parent to parent, and imparting lessons from his own life and recent reading. This low-pressure manner of conveying his opinion could incline the reader to be more receptive to Abdul's message.
- Consider how the photograph supports Abdul's argument. The image features a child fixated on a phone, ignoring the shelves of books in the background. This, in conjunction with the caption stating that 'Australian children spend hours looking at screens every day', encourages readers to worry that phones are taking up time during which children should be engaging in other, more valuable activities, such as reading books. The position of the image, placed near a list of health issues caused by screens and a reference to the risks of 'cyberbullying and exposure to adult content', invites readers to consider the potential damage being caused to this child and Australian children in general due to the overwhelming amount of time they spend on screens.

Scenario 17: Overtourism

Instructions

- In this section, you are required to analyse the use of argument(s) and language to persuade an intended audience to share the point of view expressed in an unseen persuasive text.
- Read the background information on this page and the material on the following pages, and write an analytical response to the task below.
- For the purposes of this task, the term 'language' refers to written and spoken language, and 'visuals' refers to images and graphics.
- This section is worth one-third of the total marks for the examination.

Task

Write an analysis of the ways in which argument(s), written and spoken language, and visuals are used in the material on the following pages to try to persuade the intended audience to share the point of view presented.

Background information

Fiona Carruthers is a journalist and travel editor. Her article, reproduced on the following pages, was published in the Work and Careers section of *The Australian Financial Review*.

Overtourism: why you're the one to blame

By Fiona Carruthers

Last month, I was hiking through the wilds of Tasmania's Three Capes Track with a bunch of well-travelled people when we got talking about one of the ultimate first-world problems: overtourism. Would any of us go to Barcelona, Paris or Venice ever again? 'Heavens no,' we cried into our rye three-seed crackers. (OK, maybe to Rome in the dead of winter, or Lisbon in late spring.)

Far be it from us to contribute to this noisy scourge. Congratulating ourselves on bucking the trend – we were in remote Tasmania, after all – we opened another bottle of white wine.

Just out of interest, I Googled a couple of figures from the vantage point of my solitary dolomite rock with its glorious ocean views and there it was: 1.3 million tourists a year into Tassie, for 519 200 locals. Uh-oh. Suddenly, we weren't talking about the problem, we were the problem. Right there, in our Patagonia fleeces with our keep cups, cheese, crackers and spicy Mexican dip, weren't we also just cluttering up the landscape?

Tourist creep: it happens so fast, we gasped. One minute you're not looking, the next minute people are climbing all over your harbour bridge, foreigners and locals alike. At least we can charge them $168 each for the privilege. Such a silver lining – especially for the owners of Bridge Climb.

And yet this is one boat we're all in together. Whether you have a selfie stick or not, it gets you thinking: exactly who among us should agree not to travel? Bags not put my hand up first.

Slowing the tide

A number of ideas are circulating as to how to slow the tourist tide, one of the latest being a report from the United Nations World Tourism Organisation (UNWTO) to help cities manage the impact of tourism.

Launched at the seventh UNWTO Global Summit on Urban Tourism held in Seoul, the report fleshes out the 'complex issue' of overtourism and argues that solutions, particularly in major cities, must be forged by residents and tourists – a good point when you consider that most of us fit both descriptions at some point.

We also like to blame social media, the gig economy and low-cost travel providers for this whole less-than-postcard-perfect mess. But isn't it inherent in human nature to wander, pose, paint and photograph, then return home with the victor's spoils? (Even if it is a Louis Vuitton knock-off fake-leather coin purse from Kuta's night markets.)

Before Facebook, even cavemen grunted about the better views from the caves down the road.

Nor do we learn our lesson. The ancient Greek travel writer Pausanias refers to Athens' crowds, and in the 1270s, Marco Polo had to navigate traders, travellers and bandits on the often busy Silk Road. By 1908, the concept of the annoying tourist was so apparent, British writer E.M. Forster built a novel around the theme in *A Room with a View*.

Forster writes of Florence residents pitying 'the poor tourists not a little – handed about like a parcel of goods from Venice to Florence, from Florence to Rome, living herded together in pensions or hotels, quite unconscious of anything that is outside Baedeker [travel guides], their one anxiety to get "done" or "through" and go on somewhere else'.

'The result is, they mix up towns, rivers, palaces in one inextricable whirl.'

Sound familiar? A paper by think tank Tourism Recreation Research groans that mass tourism 'is not a new phenomenon but a process that has characterised human behaviour for many centuries'.

The only real difference is that discount airlines have made it cheaper to get there.

Whether we do it for social media or noble self-improvement is irrelevant; it seems we are hardwired to hunt down fine Egyptian cotton sheets and overpriced food, preferably with a view of the Mediterranean.

In Australia, even the tyranny of distance is no longer. It's just that no one can quite decide if that's a good or a bad thing. We all need to rethink the concept of why and how we travel – and especially how frequently.

Appeal of the staycation

As a colleague who has lived abroad and speaks fluent Russian and Japanese recommended to me the other day, the staycation has rarely looked so appealing. 'You know,' he said, 'I watch all these people flying around the place – to Nepal, to the Andes and other exotic destinations – and I think, why don't you stay home? Go for a bushwalk or to the beach?'

I nodded agreement. But walking back to my desk, I suddenly wanted to ask exactly which beach, bushwalk or secret pathway he knew about, because that's what us humans do – we get ourselves in the know, be it the NSW south coast, Saint-Malo or Siberia.

Finally, for all those like me who (I'm horrified to admit) publicly lament overtourism while quietly trying to get in ahead of the pack, this was the most useful link I found while researching this column: '15 Cool Places you might not know exist in Australia'.

Lake Hillier, brace yourself. I'm coming for you next.

Tips

- Consider the publication in which this piece appeared, as well as the specific section – the Work and Careers section – in which it was included. What might be the characteristics of the typical reader of this section of this particular publication and how might this affect the way in which they respond to Carruthers' argument?
- Carruthers' tone is humorous and self-deprecating, as she acknowledges that she and her friends, despite their criticisms of overtourism, are also guilty of 'cluttering up the landscape'. Her description of their clothing and food draws on a popular stereotype of socially aware middle-class travellers; this ability to poke fun at herself and to recognise her own hypocrisy is intended to position readers to feel that Carruthers is both honest and down-to-earth, inclining them to trust her.
- The piece uses a problem–solution structure, outlining the nature of the issue before proposing the solution: the staycation. The use of subheadings helps the busy reader to understand this approach easily and to locate key points.
- Throughout the piece, inclusive language and references to broadly familiar experiences (such as buying a knock-off designer bag in Bali) work together to characterise overtourism as a shared problem for which readers bear responsibility just as the writer admits she does. In the paragraph detailing historical complaints of overtourism, Carruthers extends this idea to present overtourism as a problem of humankind itself, asserting that it is something 'we are hardwired' for. The overall intended effect is to avoid blaming readers, but also to encourage them to feel some guilt and to recognise the issues caused by overtourism, and therefore to feel as though they should do their part to fix the problem by taking Carruthers' advice.

Scenario 18: Mobile phones and jaywalking

Instructions

- In this section, you are required to analyse the use of argument(s) and language to persuade an intended audience to share the point of view expressed in an unseen persuasive text.
- Read the background information on this page and the material on the following pages, and write an analytical response to the task below.
- For the purposes of this task, the term 'language' refers to written and spoken language, and 'visuals' refers to images and graphics.
- This section is worth one-third of the total marks for the examination.

Task

Write an analysis of the ways in which argument(s), written and spoken language, and visuals are used in the material on the following pages to try to persuade the intended audience to share the point of view presented.

Background information

The following article, published in *The Sydney Morning Herald*, was written by Wendy Squires. She is a journalist, author and media consultant.

The jaywalking phone zombie plague is completely out of control

By Wendy Squires

Talk about an easy tenner. It was practically in my pocket already when I spotted a young guy with headphones in and phone in hand, walking along the street towards an intersection while I was driving with a friend. 'Ten bucks he won't look or even slow down before he crosses,' I challenged my mate, a man who prides himself on being far less cynical than I.

Gullibly, he took the wager. As if on cue, the bloke on the street stepped down from the footpath onto the road without breaking his stride or looking up from his phone. And while I was happy with money for nought, a large part of me wished I had lost the bet.

Because adding to my belief that I am now officially a cranky old woman is my obsession of late with oblivious pedestrians – especially those transfixed on their phones, in my mind yet another example of the self-obsessed and entitled today who do not care about anything other than their immediate gratification, happily ignorant of spatial awareness. Forget the rest of us and our needs and rights. We simply do not exist.

Before mobile phones infiltrated society and dictated our lives, the annoying behaviour of pedestrians not paying attention to road rules was known as jaywalking and it remains the legal term for the offence today. (Before cars dominated our roads, pedestrians would refer to bad motorists as jay drivers.) The label is generally related back to the chatty jay bird in North America, and in the last century became a slang term for a stupid, gullible, ignorant, or provincial person. New York locals began calling tourists to their town jaywalkers, as they would often roam into the middle of the road to look at skyscrapers.

Today, however, there are other terms for pedestrians who flout our road rules, many unpublishable (well, the ones I've made up are, anyway). The accepted name for those who use their phones while walking today is wexter (walker and texter), and in Australia, studies show this to be as many as one in three pedestrians.

It is this distraction that is credited as resulting in a noticeable increase in the number of those travelling by foot being injured and/or killed – around a 10 per cent increase in the United States, Britain and Australia since 2010. And this is despite the fact that this act is actually an offence according to most road laws.

I know I have nearly hit a couple of meanderers who have walked on despite red lights, turning traffic and being old enough to know better. And despite their near brush with my Mini and me, these pedestrians were so immersed in their black mirrors they remained unaware of how close to danger they were, continuing on blissfully ignorant and self-immersed. This is despite the fact 1100-plus pedestrians are injured each year on Australian roads, with these figures rising rapidly.

In 2016, in-ground lights were installed at busy intersections in Sydney and Melbourne to stop mobile-phone zombies walking into oncoming traffic. This followed efforts of other major cities in regard to the same problem, such as Paris. After the deaths and injuries of 4500 pedestrians in traffic crashes in one year alone, the Road Safety Authority of Paris introduced a Virtual Crash Billboard at some of its danger hotspots.

When a pedestrian crosses while a light is red and a 'billboard' is present, the screeching sound of a car braking to avoid impact is heard and a photo of the jaywalker's reaction taken. These photos of pure terror are then displayed on billboards all over the city as a deterrent to others.

And frankly, I think it's time we investigate having the billboards installed here. Because something needs to change and it needs to happen now.

Or, perhaps we could go one further and follow China's lead. At a crossing in Daye, a city in the province of Hubei, police set up nifty machines that warn jaywalkers not to cross when the light is red. Should they proceed, these contraptions spray water vapour at the pedestrians while photographing their reaction. These photographs are then displayed for others to see as well as being sent to police for recognition purposes.

Police report the machines are a real success and have saved lives, which makes sense considering the fear of potential water damage to precious phones may be the only way to actually motivate wexters to concentrate.

I am lucky. I do not have a love of my phone. In fact, I happily turn it off for long periods each day when I walk my dog, much to the constant annoyance of my friends. But I refuse to apologise. This is my/our precious time of carefree contemplation and exercise, a break to unwind and rewire. A time to turn off all the white noise and hear the birds instead. To listen to the jays, not behave like one.

Tips

- The writer generates a humorous tone at the beginning of the piece, with her opening anecdote followed by the self-deprecating description of herself as a 'cranky old woman'. She returns to this tone and this persona at the end of the piece, when she declares her refusal to apologise for turning off her phone and likens jaywalkers to chatty birds. In doing so, she hopes to present herself as likeable due to her frankness and principled stand.
- This forthrightness and relatability is furthered by her occasional use of casual and colloquial language such as 'tenner', 'mate' and 'nifty', as well as inclusive language, as in 'we simply do not exist' and 'our road rules'. The aim is to foster a connection between Squires and her readers as joint victims of irresponsible 'wexters'.
- Her tone shifts to informative with an element of humour as she explains jaywalking and the term 'wexter', before becoming serious as she presents statistics regarding the injuries and deaths resulting from this behaviour. These gradual shifts in tone allow her to make a serious argument, with some potentially distressing supporting points, less confronting for her readers, who are likely to have been disarmed by her conversational opening before having to take in the sobering facts and figures.
- References to international examples of wexting prevention in Paris and Daye are included to support Squires' call for similar measures in Australia. Wide-ranging precedents such as these convey the impression that other countries are ahead of Australia in tackling the problem, inciting a desire in readers to keep up with these progressive examples.

Scenario 19: Giving gifts, not things

Instructions

- In this section, you are required to analyse the use of argument(s) and language to persuade an intended audience to share the point of view expressed in an unseen persuasive text.
- Read the background information on this page and the material on the following pages, and write an analytical response to the task below.
- For the purposes of this task, the term 'language' refers to written and spoken language, and 'visuals' refers to images and graphics.
- This section is worth one-third of the total marks for the examination.

Task

Write an analysis of the ways in which argument(s), written and spoken language, and visuals are used in the material on the following pages to try to persuade the intended audience to share the point of view presented.

Background information

Athena and her large family have gathered for a Christmas meal together to exchange gifts. The following is a transcript of the speech Athena, a young professional woman, gave at the table while she handed out personalised cards to her family members. The image accompanying the text is a copy of the flyer Athena provided inside each card.

OK, well, since none of us could possibly eat another mouthful of Mum and Dad's festive meal, I've got something I'd like to say. First, merry Christmas to you all. I really love Christmas. It's not just about the food – though I have to say, Dad, this was your best custard yet! It's not just the traditional Lee family lawn bowls tournament (watch out, Uncle Rod, I've been practising!). Instead, as all the clichés say, Christmas is a time of giving.

This year, though, you've probably noticed that I didn't buy gifts for any of you – and not because I was disorganised. The real reason is that I've learned there are better ways to show my love for my family, and I'm trying to change my mindset. In each of your Christmas cards, you will find my present to you.

For some of you, I've made vouchers for things we can do together – I think they're called 'experience gifts'. (Spoiler: Gran, I'm finally taking you out for high tea.)

For some of you, I've made IOU vouchers for things I will do. This year I'll be weeding the garden (you're welcome, Mum); sewing (the twins will be the cutest-dressed kids at Morton Primary); and baking brownies (you're all hoping that's for you, right?!). Plus some other fun stuff.

But mostly, I've made contributions in your names to a bunch of different charities. I've thought really hard about them all, and chosen things that I hope will mean a lot to you. Hai, I think you will love knowing that your 'gift' this Christmas is school fees for a teenager in South Sudan. Jo (and Rover!), you'll be happy to know yours is a donation to RSPCA Victoria. Food banks, homeless shelters and medical aid all feature too.

Whether we are supporting communities and individuals close to home, or making connections with the global society we are part of, I think we have a responsibility to understand our privilege. I think we have a duty to share some of our financial and social wealth. Because most people aren't as lucky as we are in this family. In a country with free speech and a relatively functional healthcare system, we have plenty of food, we have jobs, we have homes, we have each other. But most of all, we have THINGS. Too. Many. Things.

It's easier than ever these days to spend money buying STUFF we don't need. Even kids without credit cards can buy online using Afterpay and Zip. We can pretty much have whatever we want. But have you thought about your carbon footprint with all that online ordering? The environmental costs of production, marketing and transport? What about ethical sustainability? What about treatment of workers – do you know who made your new handbag or your latest tech gadget? Do you know if they were paid fairly?

And aside from the moral cost of things, you know you'll spend more online, even when it looks like a bargain at first. Think about those ridiculously high fees you have to pay because you've left it too late and need express postage!

Or maybe you're shopping in person and supporting local small business? Awesome. Do it. Love your work. But have you thought about the cost of petrol, public transport or parking? Have you realised you're wasting hours and hours of your life panicking and searching for that perfect present for someone who has everything? A perfect present, by the way, that doesn't exist.

That's it. I'm not buying stuff for presents anymore.

And hey, there are extra benefits for you guys too. Nobody has to pretend they love the present I've given them. Nobody has to pretend they don't already have the exact same Bluetooth speaker at home. Nobody has to pretend they enjoy apricot nougat when they really don't. You all know what I'm talking about.

I know families who use a Secret Santa app where everyone only has to buy one gift. Sure, that's pretty cool – it's fun, and it reduces the sheer volume of presents. It means nobody is left out by accident. And it cuts out the stress about how much money to spend on cousins you don't know very well, or how many presents to give your siblings. It even cuts out the worry about giving someone something they don't want – the apps let you request specific gifts! But where's the joy in that? It's just a blatant shopping list. It's greedy. It's disgusting. It's consumerism gone mad. And it's nothing to do with the true Christmas spirit.

So that's why you won't find boxes from me under the tree for you this year. I'm honestly not judging the rest of you for buying presents – presents aren't all bad. But this was my choice for this year, and I hope some of you consider making the same choice next time you want to buy something for someone. (In your cards I've included a little flyer for one of my favourite charities, if you want somewhere to start.) I hope you at least stop and think about whether the present you are giving is really heartfelt, personal and meaningful. If the answer is no, then remember that there are always other options. And if the answer is yes – or maybe if it's just a particularly awesome present – then go for it!

Now, let's get the lawn bowls going!

Tips

- The speaker's chatty, friendly and intimate tone is established immediately through the use of the casual words 'OK, well' to open her speech. This reflects her close relationship with her target audience, which consists of family members who are likely to be comfortable with and reassured by this familiar approach. References to shared family experiences such as her father's custard and the family lawn bowls tournament similarly draw on the existing relationship Athena has with her listeners, allowing her to present a potentially challenging idea in a non-threatening and warm way.
- The emphasis on shared experiences is continued throughout the speech, for instance in the references to Bluetooth speakers and apricot nougat; she states that her audience 'all know what I'm talking about' to convey the idea that receiving unwanted gifts is a universally relatable scenario. This enlists the audience on her side by assuming their preferences and interests are aligned.
- The speaker uses a series of rhetorical questions to invite listeners to reflect on the impact of their buying choices. This is also a gentler way of encouraging her audience to consider her points than using a series of blunter statements. Given that her listeners are family, this softer approach is likely to be better received than a more forceful or combative style of argument.
- Consider how the image echoes and reinforces the speaker's argument, taking a similar approach and tone. It includes the capitalised word 'THINGS', which is a word Athena also emphasises during her speech, and similarly uses a rhetorical question to encourage readers to reflect on their gift-giving choices.

Scenario 20: Beach lessons

Instructions

- In this section, you are required to analyse the use of argument(s) and language to persuade an intended audience to share the point of view expressed in an unseen persuasive text.
- Read the background information on this page and the material on the following pages, and write an analytical response to the task below.
- For the purposes of this task, the term 'language' refers to written and spoken language, and 'visuals' refers to images and graphics.
- This section is worth one-third of the total marks for the examination.

Task

Write an analysis of the ways in which argument(s), written and spoken language, and visuals are used in the material on the following pages to try to persuade the intended audience to share the point of view presented.

Background information

The following article appeared in *Child Monthly*, a magazine for parents of young children, widely distributed in maternal and child health centres. Zan Smith, a mother herself, discusses concerns about the increasing amount of time children spend viewing electronic media on television, computer, tablet and phone screens, as well as increasing rates of childhood obesity in Australia.

Beach lessons

By Zan Smith

During the long wet winter we've just had, our three toddlers were cooped up in the house week after week, rarely able to escape for a run or a climb. Despite our best efforts to come up with activities and games, there was no end to the arguments and squabbling, or the constant demands for attention and novelty throughout the day.

Occasionally we resorted to the TV for half an hour or so of entertainment – and half an hour of peace and quiet in the house to get dinner prepared. But it always seemed to reduce them to a kind of inertia, stopping them from interacting with one another and from engaging in more active behaviours.

Although it freed me up to get something done, I never wanted it to go for more than an hour.

So I was very interested, and rather concerned, to read the article in the previous issue of *Child Monthly* on iPads and computers being used in classrooms from Prep onwards, to encourage kids to do their own learning and creative play – especially kids who are slow to read and write. I can't help wondering if this is all a bit too much too soon. Where is this all going? What will the implications be for our children when they are older, if interacting with a screen becomes so normal so early?

In the US, for instance, the Department of Health and Human Services has reported that 8- to 18-year-olds are watching on average around 4.5 hours a day of TV *and* spending over an hour a day playing video games. When do these children do their homework? Read a book? Play sport?

Captivated by the screen – but how much is too much?

In Canada there are guidelines for the amount of activity young children should be doing, based on findings that children aged 4 and under are spending over 70% of their days being sedentary. These guidelines are also addressing alarming levels of childhood obesity, with around a quarter of Canadian children being overweight or obese.

Is this where we're heading in Australia, too? In a country where kids used to grow up playing sport for hours after school, either in organised competitions or impromptu games of backyard cricket? Or practically living at the beach all summer? It seems the answer is 'yes'. The Australian Bureau of Statistics reports that, in 2022, 27.7% of children aged 5 to 17 were overweight or obese.

And in Australia, too, authorities are recommending lower levels of screen time for young children. The Raising Children Network recommends no more than an hour a day of screen time for children between 2 and 5, and no more than two hours for children aged 5 and over.

It's not that screen time by itself is necessarily a bad thing, in the way that eating sugar is bad for your teeth. There are many educational games and apps that kids find fun and engaging, and which undoubtedly help them to learn. And digital literacy is going to be more and more important in our children's lives.

Rather, it's the things that are not happening while you're sitting or lying in front of a screen that make it essential to limit its use. It's the senses that aren't being engaged: while sight and sound are active, taste and smell are totally dormant. Touch can be used minimally for a tablet, but there is really nothing especially tactile about a glass screen, and we all know how much children learn by doing things with their hands.

It was a great relief to our family, then, when the warm weather finally arrived and we could set off for our local beach once again, buckets and spades, towels and togs in hand. Miraculously, the arguments and demands stopped almost instantly as the fresh air, the soft sand and the cool water provided all the stimulation needed for hours at a time. Sandcastles were built, races were run along the beach, faces were splashed. There were so many things to see and hear, but even more importantly there were things to taste, smell and – most of all – touch.

The beach can be much more than a playground; it's also a school for life.

I was amazed by the transformation in my children's behaviour, from cranky to content, from depending on me as the source of all entertainment and education to finding these things readily available on the beach. The beach is not just a playground; it's also a place where children learn without even trying. Marine and bird life are all around, from seagulls to tiny fish in the shallows to the tenacious mussels, limpets and crabs eking out an existence in rock pools. Playing with water and sand becomes a lesson in flow, absorption, textures. A surfboard left on the beach for communal use becomes a child's first ecstatic experience of buoyancy.

Even the hazards of the beach are instructive: the dangers of too much sun exposure; the risk posed by creatures that might bite or sting; the threat implicit in deep or rough water. All are part of life's complexity, yet become sources of learning and understanding when they are part of an environment we clearly belong to.

So here's looking forward to a long summer, to days on the beach, to swimming lessons – and, in all weathers, the open air, the world of the senses, and sources of childhood contentment that enrich all of our lives.

Tips

- As the opinion piece appears in a magazine called *Child Monthly*, its target audience can be presumed to consist primarily of parents. Reflect on the way in which the description of a winter spent indoors with squabbling children is likely to be familiar to such an audience, whose empathetic response to this scenario primes them to accept Smith's reflections on screen time.
- The emphasis on learning through outdoor play in the latter part of the piece capitalises on this receptivity, focusing on the assumed desire of most readers, given their interaction with a parenting magazine, to wish to maximise their children's educational experiences.
- The writer generates a reflective and lyrical tone through the use of carefully chosen words and phrases; for example, the words 'miraculously', 'transformation', 'amazed' and 'ecstatic', with their connotations of wonder and even the divine, help to paint an idyllic picture of children at play. Adjectives such as 'fresh', 'soft', 'cool' and 'warm' reinforce the benefits of tactile engagement with the beach environment that the writer extols, helping to evoke in the reader a strong desire for their own children to experience the same joy and developmental benefits of outdoor time.
- Note the way in which the two images are intended to work in tandem to present a 'before and after' scenario. The former shows the backs of two young children watching a screen; the fact that their faces aren't shown both suggests that screen overuse is a problem that is not specific to these particular children but experienced by many, and creates an impression of passivity and stagnancy, given their facial expressions cannot be seen. The lighting, too, is flat and the environment in which they are sitting is drab. In contrast, the latter photo shows two happy children actively engaged in building a sandcastle. They are active, rather than sitting still, and the environment around them is rich and stimulating.

Scenario 21: Don't ban the exam

Instructions

- In this section, you are required to analyse the use of argument(s) and language to persuade an intended audience to share the point of view expressed in an unseen persuasive text.
- Read the background information on this page and the material on the following pages, and write an analytical response to the task below.
- For the purposes of this task, the term 'language' refers to written and spoken language, and 'visuals' refers to images and graphics.
- This section is worth one-third of the total marks for the examination.

Task

Write an analysis of the ways in which argument(s), written and spoken language, and visuals are used in the material on the following pages to try to persuade the intended audience to share the point of view presented.

Background information

University lecturer Bronwyn Leigh wrote the following opinion piece in response to a recent call from some parents and educators to stop using exams to assess students' skills in Year 12. Her piece was published in *Learning Now*, a monthly magazine aimed at teachers and other educational professionals.

Don't ban the exam

The exam: still a fair and accurate way to assess students

Exams. The very word has struck fear into generations of students. I well remember sleepless pre-exam nights, the long, isolating rows of single tables and chairs and the initial panic that would temporarily blank out all knowledge of a subject as I opened the exam paper. Perhaps these recollections should make it easy for me to endorse recent calls to cease using examinations as a formal assessment tool for Year 12 students. However, I'm not so sure that other forms of assessment alone help us to adequately measure student knowledge and ability. I'm also not convinced by claims that exams are as outdated as some commentators would have us believe. Of course, I'm not suggesting that exams should be the sole form of student assessment in Year 12 – or, indeed, at any level – but I do believe that they have their place and that they enable assessors to gauge student learning in a fair and rigorous way. A balance between exams and other forms of assessment is what is needed to ensure deep learning and parity of assessment.

It is worth noting that the push to eradicate exams for Year 12 is supported by very little research. No doubt most of us can guess some of the claims made against exams: that they unfairly discriminate against bright students whose anxiety hinders their ability to do well; that they are an unnatural form of assessment because no one really has to work under exam pressure in the 'real world'; and that they allow for cramming rather than deep learning experiences. There is a little merit in all of these claims – we all know of someone who didn't perform as well as they were expected to because they had a meltdown before walking into the exam room, for instance.

But these claims alone do not justify calls to abandon a form of assessment that has been reliably used in education since the mid-nineteenth century. And all of these claims can actually be used to promote exams rather than to condemn them. If students panic before exams, they need to be taught how to cope with stressful situations, because they are, like it or not, part and parcel of everyday life. In fact, many people do have to work under exam-like pressure in the 'real world': imagine being a doctor in the emergency section of a hospital and having to say to a bloodied, distraught accident victim, 'hang on while I check my reference book'. Imagine being a teacher and regularly needing to say, 'I'll get back to you on that one' in response to student questions. And, as for cramming, well, I'd rather students cram for the moment and learn something than do zilch and learn nothing. Students who can't be bothered to prepare properly for exams are unlikely to be enthusiastic about alternative forms of assessment: at least exams give them the opportunity to focus their energies for a relatively short amount of time.

One of the alternatives mooted to replace exams is a research thesis that students could work on throughout the year. The thesis would form a major component of a student's end-of-year mark, alongside usual class-based assessments. There is no doubt that engaging in such a project would allow students to develop all-important research, analytical and writing skills, regardless of the subject area. But there are a number of issues that make me sceptical about its suitability as an alternative to exams. If students needed to write, say, a 10000-word thesis for every subject, they would have very little time for their class-based studies. I also wonder how such theses – which are by their very nature highly individual pieces of research and writing – could be marked fairly and consistently for all students. And if they were marked solely by the students' teachers, what is to stop schools from exploiting the system? Even at university most students do not write a formal research-based thesis until their honours year, so it seems unreasonable to expect Year 12 students to rise to the task and for schools to have the resources to help every student achieve their best.

It is true that exams alone are not an ideal way to assess students, but in conjunction with other forms of assessment they provide a useful tool for accurately measuring student performance on a given day. My own recollections of exams are not always positive ones; nevertheless, my experience as both a student and an educator tells me that exams have their place and should not be relegated to the dustbin of history.

Bronwyn Leigh has lectured in education studies at a number of universities for more than thirty years.

Tips

- The writer takes care to acknowledge the drawbacks of exams, for instance when she refers to her own 'panic' at exams as a student and when she concedes that they are 'not an ideal way to assess students'. This serves to establish her as balanced and reasonable in her approach to the issue by suggesting that she has considered multiple angles and arrived at her viewpoint via reasoned consideration.
- The scenarios presented by Leigh – of a doctor needing to check a reference book before treating an accident victim and a teacher unable to answer students' questions – aim to alarm readers with the potential real-world consequences of not assessing students via exams. The emotive description of the doctor's patient as 'bloodied' and 'distraught' targets readers' sympathy and also their self-interest, as no one would like to be in the position of the patient under the care of an ill-informed doctor.
- Leigh's overall approach is to acknowledge that exams are 'not an ideal' form of assessment but also to lay out all the ways in which, despite this, they are still useful and ought to be kept. She does this by suggesting that many of the criticisms levelled at exams could actually be looked at as advantages – for example, they can teach students how to manage stress. She also argues that alternative methods, such as a thesis, have even more disadvantages than exams, presenting a worst-case-scenario description of a lengthy thesis requirement that would leave students little time for class-based study and raise issues of inequitable grading. The intention is to encourage readers to agree that, whatever criticisms they might have of exams, they ought to accept them as there is no good alternative.

Scenario 22: Betta fish

Instructions

- In this section, you are required to analyse the use of argument(s) and language to persuade an intended audience to share the point of view expressed in an unseen persuasive text.
- Read the background information on this page and the material on the following pages, and write an analytical response to the task below.
- For the purposes of this task, the term 'language' refers to written and spoken language, and 'visuals' refers to images and graphics.
- This section is worth one-third of the total marks for the examination.

Task

Write an analysis of the ways in which argument(s), written and spoken language, and visuals are used in the material on the following pages to try to persuade the intended audience to share the point of view presented.

Background information

Animal rights activists have long criticised pet shops for their treatment of fish, accusing them of shipping fish in cramped and cruel conditions and not caring for them when they arrive. Contrary to activists' calls for boycotts, many aquarium forums support pet shops as ethical places to buy pet fish, claiming that the fish are transported safely. Such forums also warn against shops that breed them irresponsibly.

Bettas (also known as Siamese fighting fish) don't require filters or air pumps in their aquariums and are classified as easy pets to care for, which leads to them being one of the most popular and most often mistreated fish in the industry.

The following pages feature a blog post by a mother, Rowena Soto, sharing her negative experience of buying fish in a pet shop. The post appeared on her personal blog, which usually focuses on topics relating to parenting.

Betta fish deserve betta!

So I've just been to the chain pet shop in town and I am *livid*. I've been thinking lately about getting my son a Betta, but after what I just saw I'm never going back there again!

First, they weren't even in proper tanks! Each fish was in a tiny plastic cup with hardly any room to swim or move around. They all had murky water and the poor fish were practically stacked on top of each other. A lot of them looked sick, and as far as I could tell some of them were already dead. Even my five-year-old could tell at a glance that something was wrong, asking me in a trembling voice, 'Are the fish okay, Mum?'

Of course, I hurried him away from the distressing sight, mumbling something vaguely reassuring. But the fact is, the fish are definitely *not* okay.

What are these pet shops thinking?!

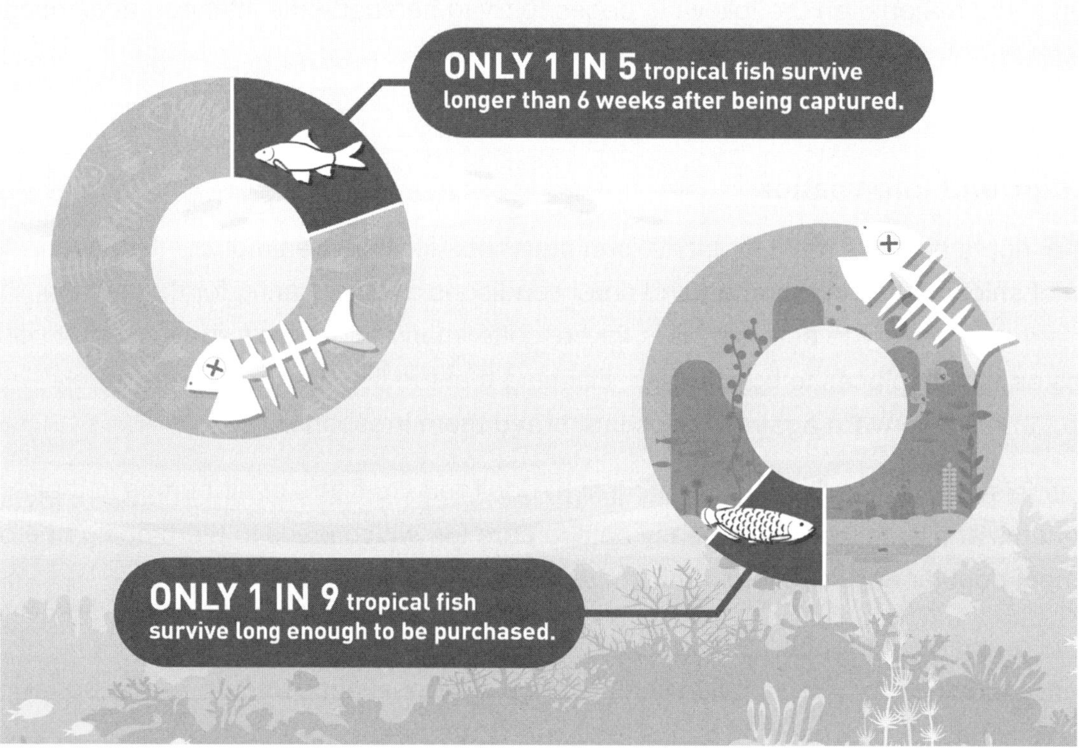

Source: https://forthefishes.org/

I tried to find someone I could talk to, but of course there were only two people working that I could see. When I complained that the fish were living in such horrible conditions, the employee just shrugged and said there was nothing he could do. Apparently they have so many other important things to take care of in this dinky pet shop that no one has time to even change the water. And on top of that, he couldn't even answer me when I pestered him about why those beautiful fish were kept in plastic prisons.

I tracked down the other employee and asked him what he knew about keeping tropical fish, and he had absolutely zero knowledge on caring for a Betta. That's when I demanded to speak to the manager, but of course she was 'not in today' so I was given a corporate phone number to call to make my complaint. The staff couldn't have been less interested in my concerns, not that I entirely blame them for their ignorance and apathy. Clearly, this lack of interest in the welfare of the animals in their care came from the top. This was not a one-off 'mistake' but a systemic issue that spoke volumes about the shop owner's passion for profit, not pets.

It horrifies me to think how many people have gone in and purchased fish with absolutely no idea how to care for them. And what bothered me just as much as the incompetent 'pet care' staff were the products being sold in the shop.

There were quite a few tanks that were labelled as aquariums for Bettas, but they were disgustingly small. Some were even designed to house several together, with nothing but a piece of plastic to keep them separated. As one of the most aggressive fish you can buy, male Bettas should not be able to see other males every second of the day, with nowhere to hide. It would be sure to cause an insane amount of stress on the fish, and stressed fish are very likely to get sick and die. Imagine being trapped in a tiny space with creatures liable to attack you at any time and no means of defending or shielding yourself. There is simply no justification for submitting any creature – no matter how small – to such psychological torment.

In the end, like my child, I had to turn away. I just couldn't believe it!

These pet shops are only concerned about one thing: money. They think that by marketing Bettas as easy pets to care for with these cute small tanks, they can make more sales. What happens to these fish after they leave the shop is clearly no concern of the owner pocketing the cash for every ill-informed sale.

After seeing those gorgeous fish in their little cups, I started to wonder if they were treated just as badly before they got to the shop. A quick internet search showed me that I was right. The fish are packed into cardboard boxes in miniscule plastic bags with a very tiny amount of water, and many of them die on the journey.

I could only stomach looking at the pictures for a few minutes before I had to turn away. Fish feel pain, people! It's been scientifically proven, and we need to do our part to help them.

So I'm asking all of my friends and followers to follow my example and never buy from pet shops again. How can a company claim to love animals when their fish are dying in transit, on the shelves and in the homes of ignorant buyers?

I almost went back to the shop to buy their whole stock of Bettas so I could rescue them, but realised there would only be new fish brought in and left to starve and rot in their own filth. I hope everyone else feels my disgust, and joins me in boycotting these unethical shops. If we don't support pet shops, hopefully they'll leave those poor Bettas alone. And you can bet I'll be calling that corporate number every day until something gets done!

Tips

- The writer generates a distressed and angry tone through such vocabulary choices as 'livid', 'horrifies' and 'disgustingly'. Such terms help to evoke similar emotions in the reader, who is thus positioned to share the writer's outrage at pet shops and their treatment of fish.
- The writer compounds this with the use of exclamation marks and rhetorical questions that aid in expressing her distress about the welfare of the fish she observed by clearly communicating her heightened emotions.
- The writer contrasts her emotional reaction with the 'apathy' of the chain pet shop and its staff: she describes them as ignorant and uncaring, with an absent manager and a 'passion for profit, not pets'. This contrast helps create an 'us and them' situation, with the writer encouraging her 'friends and followers' to align with her compassionate, more ethical point of view about the treatment of fish and to boycott the 'unethical shops'.
- While the writer's primary persuasive strategy is to target her readers' sympathy and anger, she bolsters this with some evidence to support her claims of poor treatment and ignorance on the part of pet shops; for example, when she refers to her 'quick internet search' and presents facts about Betta fish, this suggests she is well-informed on the topic. The effect is to convey to readers that her outrage is well-founded.
- The graphic included with the written text reflects this primarily emotive approach, presenting stark images of live fish alongside fish skeletons to visually present the high proportion of tropical fish deaths after capture. The statistics accompanying these images are equally stark and again reflect the writer's approach of justifying her frank distress with reference to facts and figures.

Scenario 23: Bookless libraries

Instructions

- In this section, you are required to analyse the use of argument(s) and language to persuade an intended audience to share the point of view expressed in an unseen persuasive text.
- Read the background information on this page and the material on the following pages, and write an analytical response to the task below.
- For the purposes of this task, the term 'language' refers to written and spoken language, and 'visuals' refers to images and graphics.
- This section is worth one-third of the total marks for the examination.

Task

Write an analysis of the ways in which argument(s), written and spoken language, and visuals are used in the material on the following pages to try to persuade the intended audience to share the point of view presented.

Background information

The principal of Romeo Road Secondary School, Petrov Price, writes a blog titled 'From the Principal's Corner' on the school website. He recently published the following post on the topic of bookless libraries.

ROMEO ROAD
SECONDARY SCHOOL

HOME ABOUT STUDENTS PARENTS **BLOG** CONTACT

BLOG > From the Principal's Corner

Looking back on my childhood, I have fond memories of my school library. Endless corridors lined with shelves, creaking wooden floors, cosy corners and books – so many books! There was something sacred about that building – something magical – and it came from being close to so many ideas, so much collected knowledge.

Today, however, knowledge looks a little different from when I was growing up. The new generation of digital natives associates ideas with the click of a mouse, or the results of a search, rather than the pages between two cloth boards. Which leaves school libraries like the one I used as a child – products of the paper age – facing some difficult questions.

What does the library for the digital age look like?

What does it do? And who is it for?

Romeo Road library isn't immune to these questions. Since its founding in 1945, our school has prided itself on being at the forefront of change. Ours was one of the first schools in the country to introduce the PC to classrooms in the late 1980s; we have since led the way in adopting new technologies, from BYO devices to our e-learning platform.

But despite our efforts to bring this school into the twenty-first century, our library remains firmly stuck in the nineteenth. Apart from a lone computer lab, it continues to function as a place to house physical books – a notion that is now as outdated as the atlas (remember those?), and just about as useful to our students. (Records show that students checked out just 45 books this month.) For my part, I believe it's time we close the book on Romeo Road library's dark ages – and the first step is getting rid of our collection of paper books altogether.

A library without books? It's controversial, sure – but it's not *that* controversial. Around the world, libraries are reading the writing on the screen and phasing out physical books in favour of digitised collections and electronic subscription services. At its heart, the move towards 'bookless' is about making information as quickly, easily and widely accessible as possible. Finding what you need in a traditional library means searching for the book you're looking for (or asking a librarian), taking it to the counter, checking it out and returning it; reading the ebook version of a publication, however, is as simple as searching an electronic catalogue on a device and hitting download.

And despite the term, a bookless library would actually give students access to more books than they have ever had before – including leading magazines, journals and newspapers from around the world. Phasing out physical books also has a number of other benefits, not least among them reducing the cost to an institution.

As principal, I can tell you that managing a collection of physical books is an expensive exercise: paper books require a significant amount of space and maintenance, and printed information can quickly become outdated. Ebooks, on the other hand, are cheaper than their hard-copy counterparts and accessible from anywhere with a login and an internet connection. Removing physical books and their shelves from the Romeo Road library would also create a lot of extra space, and this kind of real estate could be put to good use – in the form of extra computer labs, for example; a makerspace; or even a digital recording studio.

An additional benefit of bookless libraries that became very apparent during Covid times is that they are obviously far more hygienic. Passing any kind of physical object from hand to hand, particularly one as permeable and prone to collecting dirt and germs as a book, is just an extra avenue of risk that there seems no good reason to take if we don't have to.

Moreover – another relief for busy parents! – no borrowing of physical books means no more having to constantly remind your children to return them.

As parents and educators, it's easy to be nostalgic about libraries such as the ones we grew up with. But those libraries belonged to a world that no longer exists. Our children feel very differently about the best way to gather and store vast amounts of information, and our chief purpose here is to meet their needs and help to fit them for a digital future that will look vastly different from the one imagined when we were young.

I know how upsetting the idea of a library without books will be for some people, but to my mind the choice is clear: either we turn the page on the physical book now, or we end up having to do it later anyway. The world is changing, and Romeo Road needs to be changing with it – for the sake of our school and, most importantly, our students.

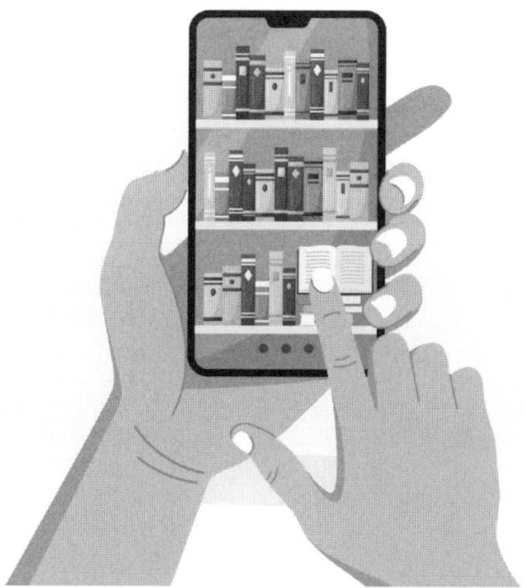

Tips

- Think about how the text's presentation – appearing on a school-branded website beneath a banner with the school name and logo on it – might affect how readers receive the principal's message, particularly as they are likely to be parents of students at Romeo Road Secondary School.
- Why might the principal open with a fond, nostalgic recollection of the library of his childhood? How might this connect him to readers and prepare them for his ultimate stance on removing physical books from the school library?
- Consider how the principal closely relates his supporting reasons and persuasive techniques to his main argument – that digitising the library is, above all, for the benefit of the students. For example, his rhetorical questions – 'What does the library for the digital age look like? … And who is it for?' – gently remind readers that, although they might have sentimental or nostalgic feelings regarding physical books in libraries, just as he himself does, this is not necessarily helpful to 'the new generation of digital natives'. Similarly, his appeal to keeping up to date and avoiding having a library 'as outdated as the atlas' is supported with the fact that 'students checked out just 45 books this month' – evidence to support the idea that contemporary students do not rely upon physical books in the same way that his generation had.
- The image the principal has chosen to include with his blog entry shows a phone screen featuring an image of bookshelves stacked with books. The suggestion is that this handheld device has the capacity to contain a large number of books, thus offering students the opportunity to read many different publications in a convenient, portable format. Consider how this might help to allay the fears of parents concerned that a bookless library might negatively affect their children's literacy and access to information.

Scenario 24: Colonising Mars

Instructions

- In this section, you are required to analyse the use of argument(s) and language to persuade an intended audience to share the point of view expressed in an unseen persuasive text.
- Read the background information on this page and the material on the following pages, and write an analytical response to the task below.
- For the purposes of this task, the term 'language' refers to written and spoken language, and 'visuals' refers to images and graphics.
- This section is worth one-third of the total marks for the examination.

Task

Write an analysis of the ways in which argument(s), written and spoken language, and visuals are used in the material on the following pages to try to persuade the intended audience to share the point of view presented.

Background information

The following article on why we should invest in establishing a colony on Mars was first published on Science is Super, a website aimed at making important scientific research, and opinions relating to scientific developments, accessible to a general audience. The author, Natasha O'Meara, is a scientist and she is a regular contributor to the website.

Three big reasons to colonise Mars – number three might surprise you!

By Natasha O'Meara

Mars holds a special place in our collective psyche. Books, films and TV shows have all grappled with the idea of a sort of interstellar Manifest Destiny, a fundamental need to go beyond the confines of our current home for the sake of our species. The lure of Mars is undeniable. So why deny it?

Some of the greatest minds of their age, from Stephen Hawking to Carl Sagan, have expressed their support for colonising Mars. At a recent meeting in Houston, the centre of space research, sixty prominent scientists who are experts in their fields reached a similar conclusion: colonising Mars isn't just a flight of fancy or a project for the distant future; it's a necessity, a vital step for humanity to take.

Of course, it's understandable there's a certain reluctance to commit to a project like this. The cost could be in the billions, trillions even, a scale of spending that's difficult to comprehend for most people. Why not spend this money on tangibly improving the lives of people now, instead of on some far-off goal that won't bear fruit for a long time, if it does at all?

But Mars missions would have practical benefits now and well into the future. Here are three reasons humans should colonise Mars.

1. The future of our species could depend on it

Experts agree that relying solely on Earth to sustain and maintain our continued existence is a recipe for disaster. The reality is that humans have been on Earth for a fraction of its existence: the blink of an eye, in a cosmic sense. Even with our limited knowledge, history is littered with examples of species coming and going; the dinosaurs, for instance, were wiped out by an asteroid.

If we could escape our home planet, however, we would drastically increase our chances of survival. And this wouldn't just safeguard against external threats like asteroids. It would also prevent us from destroying the only planet we have ever called home.

And the best part is, we don't even need to go trawling through galaxies trillions of light years away, desperately searching for somewhere habitable; Mars is right next door. Many scientists agree that Mars would make a perfect place for sustained human life; it meets many of the criteria we would want our future home to meet. By colonising it, we would guarantee that the human race will endure. And if we know all this, is there any reason not to devote our resources to doing so?

2. There could be alien life

Have you ever contemplated the existence of aliens? I think almost all of us, at one point or another, have wondered what it would be like to discover tangible proof of alien life. It would represent perhaps the most important scientific breakthrough of all time.

Of course, to properly search for life on Mars, it's vital that we get people up there. While it can be tempting to assume that we're better off letting robots do our dirty work, in reality humans are far better suited to discovery than even the best spacecraft explorers. If we want to plumb Mars' depths for its secrets, we've got to start getting people there.

There's even conjecture that life on Earth originated on Mars. Scientists have suggested that life may have come here from there via interstellar debris, such as rocks. These rocks may have contained early life and, jettisoned from their original home, come to Earth.

Unfortunately, there's been no concrete evidence found on our planet to support this theory. If anything, however, this just further intensifies the need to properly explore Mars. While we have yet to see signs of extraterrestrial life, there's every reason to think that we're simply looking in the wrong place – or planet.

3. It could materially benefit life on Earth now

Far from being a distraction from bettering life for everyone on Earth, efforts to colonise Mars would provide substantial benefits for our day-to-day lives here and now. That's because extending the limits of our horizons and striding forth into space are likely to lead to discoveries that will improve life on Earth. Pouring resources into the colonisation of Mars needn't be thought of in terms of how it might one day help us; it can benefit us much more immediately. Scientific history is full of examples of such breakthroughs.

Take, for instance, the microwave. Originally called the Radarange, the microwave's invention stems from an accident. A radar technician experimenting with electromagnetic waves stumbled upon an incredible discovery – these electromagnetic waves could be used to heat food. A now indispensable household item was the result of advancements in a seemingly unrelated field.

It's one of many life-changing discoveries that have come about as a result of humanity's drive to push itself to its limits. This story perfectly demonstrates the overlap between various fields; advancements in one area invariably benefit many others.

Moreover, not only will these myriad advancements likely prove beneficial to our health and wellbeing, they also provide us with fuel for our hopes and dreams. As demonstrated by the growing number of scientists investing time and effort into making the colonisation of Mars a reality, the prospect of being part of future space expeditions looms large in the minds of many. This could prompt future generations to take a similar interest, increasing the number of talented individuals dedicating their time to helping secure humanity's future.

The above reasons should illustrate why it's vital we commit now to going to Mars. The benefits are undeniable. So why wait?

Tips

- The background information indicates that this material is published online. Note how the writer uses a typical 'clickbait' strategy in the title of her piece, stating that 'number three might surprise you'. This is designed to encourage people to click on the article and read through to the end to discover the allegedly surprising 'big reason'. This strategy also supports the targeting of a broad audience interested in, yet mostly not experts in, science.
- The image centres on a human form on a different planet, illustrating the colonisation of Mars that Natasha O'Meara deems necessary. Consider the impact of using an image that only shows the back of the human, rather than the face. This enables the author to position the colonisation as a purely human endeavour, rather than one specific to a particular race or gender. Readers, regardless of their background, are thus able to envisage themselves as being in that spacesuit on Mars. In this case, the absence of specific identifying physical features in the photograph assists O'Meara in appealing to a wider audience.
- Consider the effect of O'Meara's ordering of the reasons for colonising Mars, and how these reasons work to position readers. As noted above, the title suggests that the third reason is the most significant, and it is certainly the most tangible and relatable to readers. The first two reasons are more aspirational or future-focused – while the survival of the human race and the possibility of alien life may attract keen scientists, an actual present-day benefit to life has the potential to connect with a wider audience.
- The article is published on Science is Super, so consider the target audience. Given the specific focus of the website, it is likely that the majority of readers have an existing interest in, and knowledge of, science. However, the article is not aimed at an intellectual or highly specific audience, as the language and content are still straightforward and accessible. Note how O'Meara includes references to two well-known scientists, Stephen Hawking and Carl Sagan.

Scenario 25: Vegan shoes

Instructions

- In this section, you are required to analyse the use of argument(s) and language to persuade an intended audience to share the point of view expressed in an unseen persuasive text.
- Read the background information on this page and the material on the following pages, and write an analytical response to the task below.
- For the purposes of this task, the term 'language' refers to written and spoken language, and 'visuals' refers to images and graphics.
- This section is worth one-third of the total marks for the examination.

Task

Write an analysis of the ways in which argument(s), written and spoken language, and visuals are used in the material on the following pages to try to persuade the intended audience to share the point of view presented.

Background information

Veganism is widely promoted as a healthy, ethical and environmentally conscious lifestyle choice. Some people argue, though, that not all vegan products are ethically superior to their non-vegan alternatives. The following article exploring the issue of vegan shoes was written by Tanner Bowden. He is a staff writer for the New York–based lifestyle magazine *Gear Patrol*.

If You Think Your Vegan Shoes Are Saving the Planet, You're Wrong

By Tanner Bowden

I have beef with vegan shoes.

Vegan leather shoes from mushroom mycelium and samples of vegan bio leather.

Let me be clear, though – I think vegans are heroes. Their personal choice not to consume animal products is literally saving the world. Veganism is hard, too. I know this because after watching the popular (though rightly criticized) documentary *The Game Changers*, which extols the benefits of a vegan diet for athletic performance, I gave it a shot for a few weeks. I wanted to see how a short-term switch would make me feel, and how difficult it would be (good, difficult, though not as much as I'd imagined). So no, my problem is not with vegans – it's with vegan shoes.

How can a shoe be vegan anyway? Simply put, it has to be completely free of animal products. That includes leather, wool and fur, as well as some glues that have animal-based ingredients in them (typically, it's collagen). Some definitions go further, insisting that any materials developed with animal testing must be excluded too.

Vegan shoes are becoming increasingly easier to find. The online retailer Zappos has a vegan filter that turns up hundreds of options from brands like OluKai, Saucony, Merrell, Dr. Martens and more. Adidas recently made waves when it revealed a vegan version of its popular Stan Smith shoe, the first iteration of which was a collaboration with Stella McCartney.

If lessening animal cruelty is the primary motivation behind your veganism, these shoes achieve that goal. But if general sustainability is the aim – and nearly every vegan shoe comes with a message that it's greener and better for the environment – the situation is messier.

The problem is that faux leather and fur are often made of synthetic, petroleum-based materials like polyvinyl chloride (PVC) and polyurethane (PU). Essentially, they're plastic. Technically, the cheap plastic-and-foam flip flops that wash up on beaches around the world are 'vegan'. Plus, in pursuing a degree of similarity that'll make people want to wear these shoes, companies often apply harmful chemicals that make them look and bend and wear just like the real deal.

OluKai is one brand that acknowledges the issue, though many don't. In a blog post on its site explaining vegan shoes, the brand notes: 'It's important to remember that animal-free shoes are not always more "environmentally friendly" by default … It is a lengthy and contentious debate as to whether leather production or synthetic production is worse for the environment.' It does note too, however, that vegan shoes are 'generally considered to leave a smaller carbon footprint'. Most companies making vegan shoes are content to greenwash over such nuance.

This conundrum calls to mind the recent implementation of plastic straw bans. I watched cafes react to it in New York City, some of them opting for paper replacements though many went for sippy lids made of plastic. Some are recyclable, supposedly, though good luck finding a recycling bin in Manhattan.

Some cafes and cities were better equipped for the ban than New York, and some companies make vegan alternatives more responsibly than others. Leather provides the best examples: an Italian company called Frumat makes it partially out of apples, while Piñatex is leather made of pineapple leaves. Mushroom-based leather is also a thing (and both Adidas and Stella McCartney will be its earliest adopters). It's promising stuff, but none of these faux leathers are being produced at a scale approaching that of the petroleum-based alternatives.

Meanwhile, is genuine leather really so bad? Again, advocates for animal rights will answer yes. From a sustainability perspective, the issue lies in the tanning process, which produces wastewater sludge with high concentrations of harmful chemicals like chromium and glutaraldehyde. Not only is it bad for the environment, but it's dangerous for those working with it.

But leather production is getting eco-friendlier too. It's a byproduct of the meat industry, for starters, and beef farmers aren't going to stop raising beef cows simply because they can't sell their skins (unless way more people adopt vegan diets, that is). Vegetable tanning uses organic material instead of chromium to preserve the skins, and some companies like Ecco are developing dry tanning methods that eliminate water waste. There's even a consortium of brands, retailers and producers that aims to hold the industry to a set of environmental protocols.

The best example of sustainably produced leather footwear comes, unsurprisingly, from Patagonia. In late 2020, the company released the Wild Idea Work Boot, made of bison leather with a Goodyear welt so the outsole can be replaced years into its life. The hides come from the same animals that it harvests to make its buffalo jerky – they are raised in a manner that restores the grasslands and promotes carbon sequestration. Previously unused, the hides are tanned with olive tree leaves. What's more, Patagonia is only making as many boots as it has enough leather for (so good luck getting a pair).

It is true that Patagonia's bison boot model doesn't scale, but neither does the mushroom leather option (at least, not yet). Sustainability is complicated, and it can feel paralyzing when it seems like every option is bad.

There is hope, though – both vegan and non-vegan footwear is getting more sustainable. And, recently, Adidas and Allbirds announced that they are putting competition aside to create a performance shoe with the smallest carbon footprint ever. Given that the latter brand's signature ingredient is wool, chances are it won't be vegan.

Tips

» Note how the writer engages the audience by using a conversational tone in the opening paragraphs. From the humorous use of the word 'beef' (employing a second meaning of the word) to the inclusion of his personal experience of, and response to, veganism, Bowden immediately softens any negativity that may have been aroused by the implied criticism in the title of the article. Both vegan and non-vegan readers are welcomed in this discussion. The tone then shifts to become more informative as Bowden introduces specific evidence to support his argument.

» Discuss the structure of the article. Bowden begins by defining vegan shoes then acknowledges the common perception of veganism as a 'healthy, ethical and environmentally conscious lifestyle choice' (quote taken from the background information). He points out that, for many vegans, 'general sustainability' is the motivation behind their veganism. The problem with this position is suggested by the article's title, in which Bowden argues that it might be 'wrong' to assume that 'vegan shoes are saving the planet'. The article then explains why faux leather and fur are problematic and goes on to discuss some genuinely sustainable alternatives. After exploring these options and establishing that there is a problem with scale, Bowden suggests that if the central desire is to save the planet then sustainable animal leather may in fact be a more viable option. Consider how readers, particularly vegan readers, might respond to this suggestion.

» Consider the impact of the inclusion of particular brand names, many of which are quite 'high-end' labels – Stella McCartney, Adidas, Patagonia. What does the writer achieve by citing such well-known and well-respected designers? Consider the implied contrast between the brands that are described as being 'content to greenwash' and OluKai, which openly acknowledges the challenges.

» Explore how the image supports the idea that vegan shoes are considered 'greener and better for the environment'. The shoes in the background of the image have a very leather-like appearance, supporting Bowden's statement that manufacturers often try to make their vegan leather 'look and bend and wear just like the real deal'. The inclusion of natural and environmentally sensitive products around the shoes – mushrooms and samples of vegan leather – adds to the impression that these shoes are natural and environmentally sustainable. The image resembles a promotional photo, which implicitly illustrates the writer's argument that vegan shoes are often marketed as 'greener and better for the environment' despite the 'lengthy and contentious debate' about this claim.

SAMPLE RESPONSES

Sample response 1: Life skills in schools

In order to promote the inclusion of a Years 7–10 'life skills' class, the Student Representative Council (SRC) at Olympus High School published, accompanying their petition, an open letter titled 'Olympus High Student Representative Council needs your help!' The letter employs an urgent yet ultimately hopeful tone, contending that dedicated life skills classes would help students succeed in their professional and personal lives. The council appeals to its audience of fellow students with the aim of moving them to sign the petition, thus enabling the group to present it to the school board for approval.

From the outset, the council adopts an insistent, critical tone intended to motivate the audience to consider the outdated nature of the current school system. The piece begins with the repetition of the phrase 'something is wrong'; when paired with the use of the inclusive 'our', the phrase positions the audience to see themselves as victims of a 'wrong' and potentially harmful school system. This attack is followed by the flippant remark that 'something is wrong when students know Pythagoras' theorem' instead of 'how to lodge a tax return', suggesting that the curriculum is impractical and not useful. The SRC then supports this remark with a satirical meme depicting two shapes and makes a sarcastic comparison between learning basic geometry and how to do taxes – a humorous appeal to logic that seeks to reinforce the notion that the curriculum 'should be focusing on the skills we need to succeed'. In this way, the image and its caption work with the main text to appeal to the audience's sense of reason, as readers are encouraged to recognise the skills needed 'in the professional world' and pursue change to their curriculum accordingly. Additionally, the inclusion of the fact that 'the government recognises the importance of developing … resilience', paired with the rhetorical 'so why doesn't Olympus High?', aims to evoke guilt in the school community and, ultimately, the school board, who is responsible for enforcing the 'teaching and learning program'. By creating a dichotomy between the government and Olympus High, the SRC encourages students to view the Olympus High curriculum, with its omission of practical life skills, as outdated and potentially harmful to their 'emotional, mental, cultural, spiritual and physical wellbeing'. This suggests that damage is being done to students, evoking anxiety in the reader and reinforcing the sense that urgent change is required.

The SRC expands on its criticism of Olympus High's current curriculum, remarking that 'the school seems to think … group projects in science classes [are] enough to … develop our communication and goal-setting skills', thus positioning the audience to question the school's ability to integrate life skills into the curriculum. The phrase 'seems to think' casts doubt on the reliability and credibility of the classes, while the sharp, short, critical 'but this is not enough' positions students to become alarmed at the lack of action, evidenced by the school's failure to modernise lessons. This sense of fear, in turn, is intended to create a desire for change. After outlining the current flaws of Olympus High's classes, the council offers a solution to the lack of a practical 'teaching and learning program', proposing that 'at least once per month a dedicated class [should] be held' and that it 'could be held at lunchtime'. By proposing a solution that works with the existing curriculum, the council positions its audience to see the SRC as considered, mature and practical, developing a reasonable tone that encourages readers to trust its views.

The letter then provides some supporting evidence, in the form of statistics from the Black Dog Institute, of the need for life skills classes. Drawing on external research lends the letter a sense of authority and reliability which, paired with the use of the inclusive 'our', invites the students to see themselves as part of the cohort requiring 'practical strategies for dealing with stress'. To counter concerns the statistics will likely generate, the letter presents an image of one possible stress-management strategy. Together with the claim that such classes are 'an investment in our long-term mental and emotional wellbeing', the image of students meditating builds on an optimistic tone harnessed by the council, designed to evoke a sense of hope that curriculum change may produce 'long-term' benefits. The students in the image seem calm and peaceful, their smiling faces and relaxed postures reinforcing the association between wellbeing and non-traditional classes. The brightness of the image evokes a sense of serenity, encouraging the audience to want to share in the benefits of practices such as meditation. The claim that 'there is hope' works with the image to portray life skills classes as a positive addition to the school program: one that would provide immediate psychological benefits to Olympus High students.

Following the proposed widespread benefits of life skills classes, the SRC cites a 2019 academic study in order to strengthen its claim that parents share the desire for a revised curriculum incorporating practical skills. In this way, the letter seeks to appeal to a secondary audience – the adult members of the school board – who would be responsible for the approval and establishment of the life classes. In claiming 'our school system has not kept up' with 'modern-day economic pressures', the student council seeks to evoke a sense of guilt among school board members for failing to adapt to changing educational needs and demands, while encouraging reflection and openness to change. Through this, the committee positions the school board to deeply consider the needs and views of not only students but also the parents who enrol their children at Olympus High, thus reinforcing the notion that life skills classes would be beneficial to the school community as a whole.

In closing, the SRC addresses its audience directly in an attempt to solidify a personal connection and reinforce the idea of a shared need for life skills classes in the Olympus High curriculum. The council develops an enthusiastic and eager tone with a plea for students to receive 'the best possible opportunity to succeed', reiterating the long-term benefits of the classes. This evokes a sense of hope in readers, positioning them to view the proposal favourably. Additionally, through the direct appeal to 'ask your parents to do so too', the council pushes students to recognise that, although they may be limited by the current curriculum, they also have the power to make a positive change. This call to action is then furthered through the letter's final line, 'let's try to get at least 100 signatures', with the phrase 'at least' carrying hopeful, motivational connotations, inspiring students to take action in order to 'thrive in the adult world'.

Sample response 2: Greenwashing

Environmental activist Makena Green-Moore's presentation uses emotive language and appeals to justice to unite her audience in a common cause and to paint a picture of their collective enemy: unethical global corporations engaging in the practice of 'greenwashing' to dupe unwitting consumers. Delivered at an ethical consumerism expo, Green-Moore's talk is intended for an audience made up of those committed to, or at least curious about, adopting sustainable shopping practices. The speaker's rapport-building strategies, buoyed by her approachable tone, work to reinforce the choices of those already shopping sustainably while also gently nudging into action those who are curious about such practices.

While Green-Moore's tone throughout is authoritative, it is also welcoming and friendly. For instance, she begins with an attempt to build rapport with her audience and ends by consolidating that rapport. Adhering to traditional conventions of speech-giving, she begins by welcoming the audience, explicitly referencing the topic of her presentation and thanking the audience for their time. She thanks them again at the conclusion of her presentation, this time adding that she is available to answer questions; she is literally approachable.

Also included at the beginning of Green-Moore's presentation is an Acknowledgement of Country. This helps to position the speaker as socially conscious in the minds of her listeners. The Acknowledgement of Country also underscores an alignment between Green-Moore's contention and the values of First Nations people, the original caretakers of our environment. This works to encourage the audience to view her as a friendly advisor who is knowledgeable about environmental issues.

Thus, when Green-Moore moves on to present the familiar scenario of attempting to pick a brand of shampoo that aligns with one's values, she has already established herself as a socially conscious speaker, so the audience is well positioned to accept her suggestion that they may fall victim to greenwashing. Her emphasis on the word 'WRONG' serves to underscore how comprehensively consumers may have been conned. However, thanks to her earlier rapport-building strategies, the audience is not likely to feel attacked or as though they themselves are at fault; rather they know she is on their side and wants to help prevent them from being vulnerable.

Through her highly emotive language choices, Green-Moore creates a dichotomy between the innocent audience and evil corporations who use unethical marketing strategies to fool consumers. For example, use of the phrase 'subjected to' emphasises the powerlessness of consumers against corporations, which is further underscored by the description of corporations' practices as 'unethical'. When Green-Moore says corporations are 'not putting in the money, time and effort' to produce ethical products and asserts that they often imply eco-friendliness 'without actually having to deliver on' it, she emphasises that positive changes are within corporations' powers and they are simply failing to act.

According to Green-Moore, however, not only are the corporations lazy but their intentions are actively sinister and manipulative. For example, they use 'false labels or symbols' and 'nasty tactics'. She claims that 'clever manufacturers and marketers … convince consumers' of falsehoods, using alliteration to create rhythm and emphasis, ensuring the point will stick in listeners' minds. Green-Moore's language choices here evoke the familiar trope of good versus evil, eliciting an emotional response from the audience and encouraging them to agree with her stance and thus position themselves on the 'good' side of the debate. Using inclusive language, Green-Moore assures the audience that she and they are on the same side, absolving them of any guilt and uniting them in the fight for 'our cause'. This is reinforced by the last line of the speech – 'don't let the big corporations pull the wool over your eyes' – which ensures that the final message the audience will take away is that they must arm themselves against this enemy.

Green-Moore thus paints global corporations as the antagonists in this story, rallying the audience to condemn their manipulative marketing and lack of action in the face of threats to the environment. Audience members are therefore well positioned to accept her appeal to their sense of justice, such as when she discusses the lawsuit currently being filed against Coca-Cola – 'the largest plastic polluter in the world' – for falsely claiming its products are eco-friendly. This appeal helps to renew the audience's sense of hope: if one of the biggest companies in the world can be held to account, perhaps change is, in fact, possible. This helps to create momentum for an audience now primed to make the 'easy changes' to their shopping habits that Green-Moore suggests.

Here, the speech changes tack slightly. Having previously established that it is not consumers who are at fault, but the global corporations who engage in greenwashing, Green-Moore now puts the onus on consumers. By listening to her presentation, consumers are no longer unwitting victims but have become empowered to recognise greenwashing when it occurs. Therefore, to now 'do what is right', the audience must respond to Green-Moore's three calls to action: they must carefully study labels and be wary of vague terms, they must shop locally where possible, and they must contact the manufacturer of a product when they cannot themselves determine whether it is eco-friendly. These calls to action are reinforced by the use of phrases such as 'pay careful attention' and 'think about what terms … really mean'. To fight the enemy and align themselves with good rather than evil, the audience must arm themselves with 'extra knowledge' and keep 'a keen eye' on marketers' practices.

Both of the included images support this message. The first image shows a hand holding a pencil with its eraser tip wiping away what looks like smoke. This image positions audience members as the ones holding the metaphorical eraser, putting the power to metaphorically erase the effects of pollution and unsustainable practices in their hands. The second image shows two generic shampoo bottles whose labels rely on some of the 'nasty tactics' Green-Moore has identified, such as including 'pictures of nature, greenery and flowers' in the design. The familiarity of this type of image points to the very ubiquity of greenwashing, encouraging consumers to remain vigilant in their everyday lives. However, it also supports the hopeful note Green-Moore has established by the end of her presentation by showing that greenwashing is ultimately easy to recognise, helping the audience to feel empowered to act.

In her presentation, Green-Moore uses a confident, approachable tone and adopts the conventions of speech-giving to position herself as a friend and eco-mentor of sorts. These rapport-building strategies are supplemented with powerful, evocative phrases and various emotional appeals, which seek to characterise global corporations who engage in greenwashing as enemies that must be fought. Combining these approaches, Green-Moore's presentation appeals directly to her eco-conscious audience and encourages them to rise to her call to action.

Sample response 3: Highfield Markets

The community of Highfield is in the process of expanding and being upgraded, though some of the consequential changes are more welcome than others. In a 'bonus' episode of his podcast *Highfield Discussions*, host Ravi Nicholson makes his love for Highfield clear while also condemning the proposed demolition of the markets to make way for a new supermarket. By presenting his opinion on multiple digital platforms, he targets a wide range of demographics in Highfield's community, urging listeners to reflect on their nostalgia about the markets as well as the unsuitability of a chain supermarket in a close-knit community such as Highfield. Accordingly, he implores locals to protect Highfield against such capitalistic intrusion by remaining loyal to local businesses, in order to conserve the markets and the sense of community that they represent.

It is clear in Nicholson's opening argument, passionately conveying his sentiments about the Highfield Markets through reflecting on his local upbringing, that he is invested in promoting and preserving Highfield as a friendly, family-oriented community. His warm and familiar greeting immediately works to establish rapport with his listeners (and those reading the transcript online) and he creates interest by inviting audiences to consider 'why [they are] hearing from [him] again so soon'. Evidently, this episode is out of the ordinary, which works to both intrigue audiences and convey the seriousness of the issue at hand. Nicholson references some recent developments in Highfield that have 'been fantastic', conveying a sense of rationality as he presents a balanced view on Highfield's progress associated with its increasing population. The changes he commends, including the 'pool', 'green spaces' for 'yoga' and 'street veggie patch', all connote health and wholesomeness, contrasted with the 'lifeless supermarket chain' described later in the piece. Through this, Nicholson establishes an image of Highfield as a vibrant and outdoorsy community, which is reinforced by the first photograph. The expanse of greenery in the background is suggestive of nature and the outdoors, and thus of health and wellbeing. The day is sunny, contributing to an impression of the marketplace as idyllic, while the many people in the picture suggest wide community support for it, thus lending weight to Nicholson's argument that the markets are worth preserving. He goes on to reflect on his own childhood marketplace memories, using pathos-laden language and nostalgic imagery such as his reference to the children who would 'duck and weave between stands', the 'colourful umbrellas' and 'friendly faces' all around. Furthermore, he is 'happy' that his own children share these experiences, indicating to listeners that the marketplace is beneficial across generations and even into the future, a point aimed at evoking nostalgia and protective emotions in the reader. After firmly establishing the social value of the markets, he discusses the 'proposed demolition' – in querying whether it is for the purposes of 'revamping the markets' or a 'new community feature', Nicholson positions the audience to hope that such a drastic action must surely be for the benefit of the community.

However, an abrupt shift to a troubled and even sorrowful tone, evident in vocabulary such as 'unthinkable loss', reveals Nicholson's fears around overdevelopment and the impact of capitalism both on the general mood of Highfield and on individuals. The markets will not be replaced by something of benefit to the Highfield community, but instead by 'just another chain store'. The bluntness of this sentence creates a sense of hostility towards the supermarket, with 'chain' being used to represent its generic nature, which Nicholson portrays as completely out of sync with Highfield's unique vibrancy. Indeed, he describes the proposed building as 'a big concrete block' – such simple language conveying a sense of ugliness and harshness. Nicholson continues by making explicit the 'cost' of such a development – to the 'economy', to the 'work and wellbeing' of 'beloved' locals, and in terms of the loss of 'high-quality fresh products'. Using a list here helps Nicholson emphasise the far-reaching risks the supermarket poses to all Highfield residents, not just market-goers, thus positioning all listeners or readers as stakeholders in this issue. He also identifies individual market stallholders, pointing out that not just 'businesses' but 'people' will suffer. Through this, Nicholson humanises the markets so that audiences are more likely to rally in order to protect particular people who they value in the community. This strategy is supported by the second image, of a woman walking through rows of empty market stalls, establishing a sombre visualisation of the end of the Highfield Markets. Although the photo is of just a single person, her face is not shown, encouraging us to see her as representative of all the other individuals Nicholson previously described. The similarity in composition of the two photographs, each showing a central figure in a market from behind, highlights the contrast between the bustling, vibrant scene in the first image and the desolate atmosphere in the second, with the aim of provoking the reader's alarm and dismay.

Finally, after Nicholson has vividly made audiences aware of the risks to Highfield of condoning the proposed supermarket, he urges them to take action to 'support' the local community in order to protect against such developments. He appeals directly 'to my listeners' and 'applaud[s]' those who have already put up 'protest posters and signs', thus encouraging those who have, so far, remained bystanders to engage more with the issue by taking similar action. He advertises a 'petition link' and suggests that residents 'write to [their] local councillor', thus providing audiences with tangible, simple actions that they can take to support Nicholson's cause. He uses repetition in the phrase 'this weekend and every weekend' to emphasise the importance of consistent patronage, particularly now, 'during the hard times', appealing to the audience's sense of responsibility as part of 'a community that cares for each other'. The final reminder that Highfield is 'special' and not 'ordinary' reinforces earlier sentimentality about the markets and the locals who will struggle if the supermarket goes ahead, and firmly underlines the notion that the unique, caring, community-focused Highfield is no place for a generic supermarket.

So, by appealing to his audience's sense of nostalgia in his opposition to the demolition of the local marketplace to make way for a chain supermarket, Nicholson reminds his listeners (and online readers) of the wholesome image that Highfield represents. In doing so, he positions like-minded community members to rally behind his message in order to preserve the town as it is.

Sample response 4: Handwriting

In 'The vanishing art of handwriting', Leslie Slater argues that, although handwriting is disappearing from our lives, there is a range of reasons why it should be valued and not lost from our culture. In a mostly moderate tone, Slater uses a range of supporting arguments and strategies to convey the value of handwriting, from personal anecdote to scientific evidence. In addition, she sets out the reasons why handwriting is disappearing from our lives, emphasising the risk that a valuable part of our culture could easily be lost and thereby increasing the importance of understanding how handwriting enhances our lives.

Slater begins with a personal reflection on the pleasure of writing with a fountain pen. This opening section conveys to the reader Slater's strong personal interest in and engagement with the issue. The connection between handwriting and human qualities is subtly suggested through phrases such as 'a mirror held up to their human creator'. Later, in discussing Philip Hensher's book *The Missing Ink*, Slater favourably compares handwriting to the use of a computer. The positively loaded terms 'personal and unique' are used to describe handwriting, whereas the more neutral or negatively loaded terms 'mechanical and mass-produced' are used to describe computers. Even though Slater is clearly presenting a personal view, the close connection she establishes between handwriting and humanity positions the reader to see handwriting as something inseparable from being human, and therefore something that should not be lost.

The reference to Hensher's book also consolidates Slater's personal reflections, indicating that such thoughts are shared, particularly among those who are educated and interested in books and writing. The audience for *The Missing Ink* would have a strong overlap with that of the weekend newspaper supplement in which Slater's opinion piece appeared, which would be likely to be read by professionals looking for relaxing yet sophisticated reading material. Slater thus appeals to shared tastes and interests, inviting the reader to feel part of a community that would be interested in and concerned about the loss of handwriting. The image placed next to the discussion of Hensher's book also reinforces these sentiments, showing a beautiful fountain pen and neat, perfectly formed handwriting – items that appear valuable because of their beauty, and which the reader is encouraged to feel should be kept for this if for no other reason.

The image caption 'Beautiful handwriting: a vanishing art?' introduces the idea – also signalled by the title of the article – that handwriting is becoming much less common. Slater moves from Hensher's book to consider the education system in Australia, giving the article a specific relevance and importance in a local context. The difficulties caused by the decline of handwriting in school, especially when students do exams, are conveyed by negative terms such as 'struggle' and 'fatigued'. These words create an image of an exhausted and nearly defeated student, contrary to the more familiar image of teenagers as healthy and energetic, which emphasises the problems already being caused by the decline of handwriting. Slater does not acknowledge any positive aspects of increased computer use in schools, such as for students who find it difficult to write by hand. The omission of such a perspective encourages readers to see only the negative side of the issue, and to feel that it is inevitable that handwriting will continue to disappear from schools, and therefore from everyday life.

The image accompanying the paragraph on potential computer use in final Year 12 exams also reinforces the idea of the widespread use of computers in education. The pens and paper lie beside the computer, apparently not being used; indeed, some pages are screwed up, in what could be considered a metaphor for the rejection of the 'old' technology. Instead the hands lie seemingly relaxed on the keyboard, suggesting this is now the 'normal' way of doing work, and the pencil is simply unnecessary. This emphasises Slater's point that handwriting is disappearing, while the relatively stark and utilitarian nature of the image compared with the more gently lit and aesthetically pleasing earlier image helps to support her claim that something valuable is being lost with growing digitisation.

The use of quotations from experts gives Slater's arguments more force and weight. An experienced teacher, Kim Jones, is quoted in the paragraph on the teaching of handwriting, and later a university professor, Virginia Berninger, is quoted in the discussion of handwriting's positive effects on the brain. Here the discussion becomes more serious and the style becomes slightly more formal in such phrases as 'although it is far from clear …' This shift in tone and style emphasises the importance of this section, which provides the strongest evidence for the importance and value of handwriting.

From the strongly personal tone of the opening paragraphs, the article becomes more objective towards the end, emphasising scientific evidence and expert testimony. This positions the reader to see the issue as having wide relevance – attracting international research and discussion – and as having far-reaching implications. The reader is led to see handwriting not just as a matter of personal taste but as one of great significance for learning and thinking.

Slater concludes by creating a greater sense of urgency in the reader's mind, with the phrase 'until it's too late' conveying the need for action. This brings together the two strands of Slater's argument: that handwriting use is declining and that handwriting has great value to humanity, giving coherence and impact to the conclusion. The use of inclusive language ('we can't also keep', 'a crucial part of our minds') moves back to the more personal tone of the article's opening, while also highlighting the wide relevance and significance of the issue. This is intended to leave readers with the feeling that Slater is right to be concerned about the future of handwriting, and that they, too, are stakeholders in this issue.

Sample response 5: Penny's Petals

In a scathing attack on the global flower industry, Penelope Acosta implores her flower-loving readers to avoid purchasing globally sourced cut flowers and to buy flowers that are produced locally and ethically. In a social media post, Acosta paints a vivid and alarming picture of the global cut-flower industry. She first gives compelling evidence of the low-quality working conditions and harmful environmental impacts of this industry, then presents her own Australian business as the solution, urging consumers to buy ethically produced local flowers.

Acosta begins her post with a variety of techniques designed to appeal to and engage the interest of her flower-loving audience. An elegant 'Penny's Petals' logo adorns the top of the page and contrasts strongly with the dramatic image directly below. The black-and-white photo features a perfect rose in a bottle, with a drooping rose shadow in the background. The repeated use of flowers in the logo and the main photo clearly targets the audience of flower-buying Australians who might have found their way to one of Acosta's social media accounts, either by accident or because they already follow the florist. Combined with the headline, 'Shock in the Shop!', the black-and-white image signals the dark side of the cut-flower industry, sparking the reader's curiosity and concern. The healthy, upright flower represents the flowers sold in many shops, while the wilting shadow it casts represents the harmful reality of the cut-flower industry. Together with the sombre monochrome tones and unadorned background, the image provides stark visual support for the writer's argument that the industry is exploitative and even deceitful.

Acosta opens with an anecdote designed to appeal to her audience, presenting the question that prompted her exploration: 'where did that rose come from?' She sets the tone for the remainder of the article with playful, almost poetic language such as the alliterative 'beautiful bouquet', which contrasts with alarming words such as 'shocked' and 'sinister', establishing a dichotomy between the appeal of the flowers and the highly negative aspects of the industry that produces them.

Continuing in this dramatic and concerned tone, Acosta presents her first argument: that the global flower industry is unethical and harmful to workers. She uses a series of statistics to highlight the sheer size of the industry, from the 'US$55 billion' in revenue to the '660 million stems' sold in 2020. After establishing the enormity of the industry, she then highlights its substantial human impact through a series of highly emotive images of workers. These include descriptions of demanding '16-hour days' and the 'fertilisers, insecticides and preservatives' that are 'full of toxins', which are likely to make Acosta's readers feel that these workers are being exploited and harmed. These details are also likely to prompt readers to question the origin of the flowers they buy and the conditions in which they are produced. Acosta even discusses the broader communities surrounding the farms, creating a particularly vivid image of Ecuadorian children who have 'altered short-term brain activity' simply from having contact with workers' clothes and equipment. The writer makes it clear that the huge global cut-flower industry has a detrimental effect on the people involved, encouraging readers to reject its ethics and question their own buying habits.

After discussing the human impact of the industry, Acosta moves on to discuss the equally distressing environmental damage it causes. Her arguments have a cumulative effect, reinforced by her use of phrases such as 'it is not only ... but also' and 'doesn't even consider'. The effect is to create the impression of a large and ruthless industry causing significant, even overwhelming, harm. To reiterate her earlier points about the scale of the industry, Acosta uses words and phrases such as 'masses' of flowers, 'distributed all over the world' and 'astronomical carbon footprint'. The 'environmental toll', Acosta argues, is so shocking that it should cause anyone to question whether their purchase is ethical, to seek to know the source of any flowers they purchase, and to find alternatives to the mainstream global cut-flower industry.

Enhancing the emotional impact of her text, Acosta presents her argument as a story, moving from the time the flower grows to the moment it is purchased. Again, she amplifies the dramatic impact of her argument by using phrases such as 'harsh plastics' and 'shoved onto foam blocks … laced with chemicals'. The impression she creates in this way is of an uncaring, brutal industry that her readers are unlikely to want to support. The writer argues that the journey from overseas farm to Australian flower shop is fraught with ethical problems, positioning readers to feel that there should be an alternative.

Acosta begins the final section of her post by presenting a solution to the problems of the global cut-flower industry: her own local flower shop. Having established the reasons why flowers imported from overseas should not be purchased, Acosta argues that her 'local farm' embodies the opposite qualities. She uses terms with strong positive associations, such as 'family' and 'eco-friendly', in direct contrast to her earlier, strongly negative language used to characterise the global industry. Acosta also focuses on the 'Aussie farmers', 'beautiful Australian natives' and 'Australian businesses just like mine' to elicit feelings of local and national pride. Emphasising her use of 'recyclable materials' and 'beautiful arrangements', Acosta returns to the positive language and imagery of the start of her post in order to leave readers in no doubt that Penny's Petals is the best alternative to the 'real cost' of the overseas cut-flower industry.

Sample response 6: The wearable workplace

In his article 'The wearable workplace', published in the business publication *SuitNoTie*, Brannigan Forsythe explains to a target readership of business executives why they should invest in wearable technology for their employees. Forsythe draws on his experience as a former CEO, and on research and other evidence, to support his contention. He uses a conversational tone throughout to create an impression of an author who, although knowledgeable on the topic, is also relatable, encouraging readers to view him as trustworthy as well as informed. The article is accompanied by a cartoon that expresses a slightly opposing viewpoint on the use of wearable technology at work; however, in the context of the article, the cartoon is likely to be viewed as a humorous illustration of the topic and a complement to Forsythe's lighthearted approach, rather than as a rebuttal of his arguments.

Forsythe's background as 'the former CEO of a multinational company' establishes his business expertise, providing readers with a reason to believe his claims about wearable technology. Confident statements such as his assertion that 'the wearable technology revolution is here' and his indication that he would know the outcome of a 'quick survey of wearable tech on the market right now' create the impression that he has an in-depth knowledge of wearables, encouraging readers to trust him and believe that his support of wearables comes from a place of expertise. He bolsters this sense of expertise with references to statistics and other evidence, citing data reported by large, well-known companies Liberty Mutual and PricewaterhouseCoopers. The use of data from presumably trustworthy sources helps support his claims and acts as proof that he is deeply knowledgeable about the topic.

Having established the idea that he is experienced and well informed, Forsythe appeals to his readers' desire to stay up to date. Considering recent rapid advancements in technology, there is significant anxiety regarding how technological advancements will impact businesses, and this would be a concern to those who read *SuitNoTie*, as it is aimed at those wishing to keep up with business developments. Forsythe alludes to this context of technological change in the article's opening, which suggests that readers have been expecting a 'revolution': 'It's official – the wearable technology revolution is here'. His choice of aggrandised words regarding the technology throughout, including 'supercharge', 'state-of-the-art' and, repeatedly, 'revolution', reiterates the game-changing potential of such advancements, encouraging readers to feel that wearables will have a significant impact on the business world. At the same time, he leans on companies' potential concerns about falling behind with technology, suggesting wearables are already prolifically used: he states that 'wearables are more popular than ever'; that 'many companies can tell you' of their ability to foster health consciousness; and that 'companies all over the world are using similar tech'. Brief descriptions of the ways in which large companies Audi and Hitachi use wearable technology similarly promote this idea of a mass uptake of wearables, inviting readers to think they too should invest in wearables lest they not 'keep ahead of the curve' and, by implication, suffer financially while businesses around them embrace the 'revolution'.

Forsythe also takes on a casual tone throughout the piece. Very short informal sentences such as 'Curious?', 'Enter wearables' and 'Well, good news, folks!', alongside colloquial language such as 'tech' and 'an easy sell', contribute to an overall personable voice, as though he is writing to a friend, encouraging the reader to feel they can trust him. The headings use informal language such as puns, playing with the different meanings of 'work' or words associated with wearable items: 'Working out what fits (and wearing the consequences)' and 'Wearables that work for you'. This helps make Forsythe's arguments memorable and contributes to the article's casual tone, building an impression of Forsythe as a relatable businessperson. He furthers this impression by addressing the reader directly with rhetorical questions that guess what they are thinking: 'what does that have to do with you and your business?' and 'what would you prefer to be paying for?' This approach indicates he understands how readers are responding to his article, inclining them to trust he knows where they are coming from and to believe his contention that wearables would be beneficial to their business.

Forsythe concludes with an acknowledgement of a potential challenge to the use of wearables: employee resistance. This acknowledgement of an oppositional viewpoint serves to assure readers that Forsythe has considered different aspects of the issue, and yet has still concluded that wearable technology is worth the challenge. His solution – 'a comprehensive plan for educating employees' – also diverts from the concern of privacy, as he uses survey results to argue that the 'real issue … is trust', implying that if employers are trusted enough by their workforce, they would be able to overcome this barrier. He follows this up with another appeal to being up to date, leaving readers with the lingering image of a company that will 'watch the revolution pass them by', stating that, despite potential difficulties, 'wearables are here to stay', with the implication that readers have no choice but to embrace the change and invest in wearables.

The cartoon accompanying the article illustrates the challenge of employee resistence, showing an office worker running frantically as his watch tells him that he is fired. As with Forsythe's acknowledgement of challenges, the inclusion of this image with the article demonstrates a rounded perspective on the issue. The lighthearted cartoon format also adds a humorous touch that aligns with the article's casual tone and, in the context of Forsythe's conversational approach, minimises the seriousness of the counterargument that the image presents.

Forsythe presents himself as friendly, but experienced and informed, encouraging readers to view him as a trustworthy businessperson with a high level of knowledge about wearables. He uses this impression to position readers to believe that they can trust his endorsement of wearable technology and its potential business applications. Further, his appeals to the desire to stay up to date with technology create a sense of urgency, as, in the current climate of rapid technological advancements and change, the embrace or rejection of technology can be a deciding factor in a company's success or failure.

Sample response 7: Halloween

Redfern resident Nadia Laghari has long questioned the relevance of Halloween in Australia. In her contribution to the *Redfern Reader*, Laghari ponders the celebration and states that, while it has taken her some time, she has come to realise that it not only promotes memory-making for families, but also brings the wider community together as they find ways to celebrate the event in an Australian context. Her thoughtful, friendly tone and considered exploration of both her initial negative feelings towards Halloween and her later appreciation of it position the reader to view her argument as balanced and reasonable.

Laghari opens her piece by expressing her annoyance at the paraphernalia 'popping up everywhere' in celebration of Halloween. She commiserates with other parents that they have only 'just had school holidays' and yet it is 'too early for Christmas', taking aim at the constant stream of events for the kids to be excited about. Her lamentation continues as she outlines why it has taken her 'a long time to understand why we bother with Halloween', questioning the 'influence' of America on Australian culture. In doing so, Laghari intends to raise fellow Redfern residents' awareness of the idea that, by celebrating Halloween, families may be perpetuating the Americanisation of the nation. Additionally, she lists a range of negative associations Halloween may have for parents, including 'mass consumption of lollies', 'havoc' at dinnertime and needing to 'dole out' treats to 'a never-ending stream of strangers', using vocabulary with connotations of both greed and chaos that is likely to arouse the reader's anxiety. The inclusion of the photograph supports Laghari's stance on the 'ritual' of unhealthy treats, with the substantial amount of lollies serving as a visual representation of the 'sugary occasion'. The image conveys a sense of excess and aims to alarm readers, particularly those who are parents, about the amount of sugar being consumed by children. The way in which the sweets are spilled furthers this impression of careless overconsumption, while the inclusion of this image early in her piece vividly reinforces the writer's concerns.

However, having outlined her reservations about the occasion, Laghari then considers the positive impact that it has had on the community and her own family. The shift from her initial complaints about Halloween to promoting it, accompanied by a shift in tone from cynical to positive, demonstrates her personal growth from when she 'dreaded that haunted night' to now 'rethink[ing] Halloween'. She explains how by 'getting more involved' with the 'life it brings to the street', she now enjoys the occasion, rather than just 'tolerat[ing]' it. This acknowledgement aims to show the Redfern populace that embracing Halloween can enrich their society. Laghari illustrates this point by outlining the ways the community has embraced the custom as their own. Her reference to 'home-baked cookies and fruit' as a replacement for 'plastic-wrapped candy' positions readers to see that they can 'strike a balance' when it comes to 'naughty and nice' treats; the celebration does not have to completely revolve around the sorts of unhealthy snacks depicted in the earlier photograph. Laghari also establishes a sense of community spirit in readers by commenting on how celebrating Halloween has reconnected her family with 'neighbours we've fallen out of touch with' and enabled them to 'meet … new families'. Here, she reminds the Redfern community that 'the whole suburb' can be involved and make this event feel 'special'. Laghari's repetition of words and phrases related to 'community', with their connotations of friendship and support, suggest to the reader that, rather than being about excess, Halloween's value lies in the way it strengthens bonds between people. The reader is positioned to associate the occasion with universally positive emotions that are as relatable for Australians as they are for Americans.

In addition to referencing how Halloween has been embraced by those around her, Laghari reflects on the influence this celebration has had on her own family. Her anecdote describing the way her children have learned positive 'lessons' personalises her contention, and by highlighting the repurposing of clothes in a fun 'costume challenge', she demonstrates how Halloween can enable parents to teach their children about 'reusing and recycling' to target larger environmental issues. She attempts to elicit an emotional connection with readers, describing how she and her children 'bond over sticky tape and craft glue', inspiring readers to form their own fond memories through a family celebration of Halloween. The emotional impact is further strengthened by the photograph of three children expressing their delight in being dressed up in costumes, which helps to characterise Halloween as a fun occasion, thus validating Laghari's eagerness to participate. The photograph also depicts the sense of joy the event has brought to her family, providing her with the opportunity to connect to her children's interests, seeing 'what they've been reading and watching, and which characters they … want to dress up as'. This further supports Laghari's point that celebrating Halloween has had a positive impact on her family and, although she formerly held reservations, she now feels 'inspired … to participate'. Use of the verb 'inspired', associated with creativity and elevated emotions, aims to elicit a similar excitement in the reader, who is positioned to question any negative assumptions they themselves might have had about Halloween, just as Laghari has.

Laghari concludes her opinion piece by reminding readers that they are already enjoying 'imported' celebrations, and therefore shouldn't be criticising the inclusion of Halloween in their community simply because it originated overseas. She states that celebrating these 'rituals' embraces the 'multicultural nature of Australia', further igniting a sense of community spirit among readers to encourage them to adopt another ritual and recognise what it can bring to their lives. In her closing comments, Laghari discusses the way Australians have embraced their own interpretation of American traditions, using familiar, positive imagery in her references to beach Christmases 'rather than play[ing] in the snow' and a community-focused Halloween on 'a warm spring night', with the aim of evoking warm personal memories of such occasions in the reader. By doing so, she leads her readers to think that by putting their 'own unique spin on the occasion' they can bring a real sense of community spirit to Redfern.

Sample response 8: The Salty Boot

In a tone that is forceful, yet at times also sentimental, speaker Vince D'Angelo implores the audience to help save the iconic music venue known as The Salty Boot. His speech is part of a rally aimed at preventing the closure of The Salty Boot in response to complaints by new local residents that the venue creates too much noise. For D'Angelo, these complaints are part of a wider trend towards gentrification in older, inner-city suburbs, and he rejects the specific complaints as well as the wider cultural shift, positioning the audience to view the old venue with affection and longing. The flyer for the rally features a cartoon by Roisin McCrae, which presents a critical view of loudly protesting residents and a sympathetic view of musicians and The Salty Boot itself, depicted as being dwarfed by apartment blocks on either side. In the background are the cranes and high-rises of relentless urban development. Overall, the cartoon supports the argument presented by D'Angelo that changes in the suburb are harming the community and will lead to the loss of a unique venue that is more like a home than a business.

D'Angelo is speaking, in many ways, to 'the converted' – in other words, to people who believe and feel much the same as him. His purpose, then, is not so much to convince them to agree, as to persuade them that The Salty Boot is worth saving and that, if they all act together, they can save it. To do this, he aims to elicit strong feelings of affection for the venue, portraying it as 'a special place' that is much more than a music venue. It is a 'home' and a 'refuge'; it is safe and, like a caring friend or family member, has always 'welcomed us'. The colloquial name for the venue, 'the Boot', captures both a sense of familiarity and an appealing grunginess, reinforced by the image of 'chicken parmas that taste like tyre rubber'. This humorous description suggests something authentic, flawed and, like tyre rubber, extremely resilient. As D'Angelo's speech proceeds, The Salty Boot takes on qualities that are almost human, so that the idea of losing it comes to seem like the idea of losing a valued friend.

This strong sense of loss is reinforced about halfway through the speech, with the repetition of the phrase 'say goodbye' and a sequence of rhetorical questions that heighten the audience's feelings of bewilderment and of having something unique and treasured taken away from them. Phrases such as 'soaring guitar' and 'incredible musicality' suggest euphoric experiences, likely to evoke memories of similar experiences in the audience, while 'freedom to be themselves' suggests a high level of independence and acceptance that is not easily achieved elsewhere. D'Angelo thus increases the level of sentiment and longing, making very emotional appeals to the audience in order to strengthen their (already significant) feelings of attachment to The Salty Boot.

At the same time, D'Angelo presents the world without the Boot as a world that is antithetical to human feeling. It will be 'boring', a 'world of cool nothingness' – a world that his audience would have no desire to be part of. The image of 'band t-shirts … on walls' (as opposed to band t-shirts being proudly worn) suggests a detachment and a separation between people and the things they support, rather than a full-blooded participation in life. This world is also evoked in Roisin McCrae's cartoon, which shows residents isolated from one another in their apartments. Their near-identical windows signal the lack of individuality brought about by gentrification, while two residents who are screaming at the musicians make a mockery of residents' complaints about the music venue being too loud. The tall apartment blocks dwarf the older building that is home to The Salty Boot, which looks far more characterful and welcoming with its curved window frames and half-open door. The musicians, too, appear unthreatening and vulnerable, while the attitudes of the mother and cafe worker on the footpath are unfriendly and even (in the case of the cafe worker) aggressive, portraying a neighbourhood to which few people would wish to belong.

This contrast between 'us' (those who want to preserve the Boot) and 'them' (those who want to destroy it) is a strong feature of both the cartoon and the speech. D'Angelo uses inclusive language throughout to emphasise that he and his audience are essentially in agreement on the issue from the start, since they are all attending the rally together. In addition, those who comprise 'us' are humanised, described as having known times 'when things were tough' and as having progressed, like 'Trombone Jackson', from being aspiring musicians to achieving success and fame. The musician's offbeat name helps to personalise the issue and provide a positive human story typical of The Salty Boot's history. On the other hand, those who find 'the suburb's trendy aesthetic' appealing are simply referred to as 'they': they are nameless 'naysayers and complainers' (depicted convincingly and disparagingly in the cartoon) who seem opposed to everything D'Angelo thinks is fun.

In a shift in the argument near the end of the speech, however, D'Angelo suggests that the residents who seek to close down The Salty Boot are in fact members of his own generation. In other words, in their younger years they, too, enjoyed the 'benefits' of the Boot – enjoyable evenings of 'letting loose', good company and great music – but now they seek to deny the younger generations the same fun. In this way, D'Angelo portrays his opponents as selfish and hypocritical, weakening the strength of their arguments as he does so. Their ideas of creativity and self-expression are presented as limited in scale and ambition, at the level of 'latte art' – a metaphor for everything that is superficial and pretentious about gentrification.

Having belittled and dismissed the opposition, D'Angelo returns forcefully to his audience with a final pitch to persuade them to sign the petition and fight to save 'our Salty Boot'. Defiantly, he declares that he is 'not prepared to say goodbye' and won't 'let them pull the plug'. This clichéd expression creates a simple, easily visualised image of an electrical plug being pulled from a socket, an image that is both an appeal to fear – it has connotations of ending life-support – and a signal that effective action can still be taken. The repeated d's of 'keep our Salty Boot dark, dingy and dirty' contribute to the forceful, passionate conviction at the end of the speech, as the 'heavy heart' of the opening is finally replaced by feelings of hope and determination. Whereas the hapless musicians in the cartoon appear incapable of defending their venue, D'Angelo conveys strength and optimism to his audience, leaving them likely to feel that saving The Salty Boot is not just desirable, but achievable.

Sample response 9: Golf course development

Although the local council is yet to approve her proposal, landscape architect Alejandra Ortega makes an impassioned plea to the members of the community to gain their support for a contentious golf course development. The transcript of Ortega's speech, which includes personal yet logical language, as well as images to persuade the local audience to support her cause, demonstrates her passion for the proposal. Rather than dwell on the personal benefits to her company of the partnership with Goodgreens Developers, Ortega instead speaks positively of the benefits to the community, and plays down the loss of the old Westhaven Showgrounds. She employs an open and inviting tone throughout her speech that seeks to welcome discussion and make her audience feel as if their opinions are valued.

Ortega begins her speech with both an extremely favourable overview of the proposal and an indication of why the audience should trust her. Starting on a positive note, she uses the inclusive 'my fellow community members', coupled with heightened adjectives such as 'amazing' and 'exciting', to create a sense of community and feelings of awe among her audience of Westhaven residents. By highlighting her status as a local, which she depicts as a significant factor in her discussion through the phrases 'far more importantly' and 'a local … through and through', she invites the audience to regard her opinion as guided primarily by a strong desire for the community's collective good. She ties this line of thinking directly to saying 'yes' to the golf course proposal, framing her decision to partner with the eco-friendly-sounding 'Goodgreens Developers' as an act of 'love' for the town – a message that she repeats throughout the speech. In presenting her argument, Ortega uses extremely positive language referring to community unity, which positions the audience to view the proposal as universally beneficial and therefore worthy of support.

Shifting from her emotional basis for working with Goodgreens, Ortega peppers the next part of her speech with facts and a number of excited comments about the sport of golf. Referring to the 'ausgolf website' and an 'official Sport Australia survey' is intended to add credibility to her assertions that 'Australia has more golf clubs per capita than almost any other country' and that it is a growing sport. The audience is left with the sense that, if they do not get behind this growing trend, they will be left behind. Ortega even suggests that the rise in golf's popularity may be due in part to the COVID pandemic, with golf offering valuable opportunities for 'aerobic exercise', 'community' and improving 'hand-eye coordination'. Each of these points is punctuated by an excited exclamation of 'Golf!', leaving Ortega's audience in no doubt about her enthusiasm for the sport. This repetition highlights the multiple benefits that some in the audience may not have been aware of, thereby encouraging them to consider the sport in a new and highly favourable light.

Ortega then addresses community concerns about the loss of the Westhaven Showgrounds, arguing that the 'freely accessible' site is in decline. Despite lacking official council approval for the proposal, Ortega gives the impression that the council endorses her venture by stating that 'with the support of the council' she has conducted research showing bookings for the Showgrounds 'have declined by over 40% in the last four years'. The perceived support of the council and the use of statistics leads the audience to view her following argument as credible, logical and well-informed. Ortega's interpretation is that the community is 'not making use of the facilities' other than for 'parkrun', the playground and occasional use of the barbecue. Ortega supports this argument with an image that she sums up with a litany of negatives: 'rusting grandstand, dilapidated fencing and old toilet block'. The image employs harsh grey tones and places the ramshackle grandstand in the foreground, thereby concealing the beauty of the natural trees behind. The composition of the image thus highlights to the audience the negative attributes of the current infrastructure, positioning them to agree that a development is sorely needed. Ortega ends her criticism of the Showgrounds by commenting that upgrading the free facilities would require 'new and sustainable revenue streams', leaving the audience to wonder where the money could come from, and making the idea of retaining the current facilities seem untenable.

Immediately proposing a solution to the disrepair of the Showgrounds, Ortega proceeds to argue that private development of the golf course is the way forward for the town. Her subsequent image replaces the worn-down grandstand with a bright picture of two children playing golf. The sun shines on the well-dressed children, glinting off the clubs in the foreground. The course is well manicured, in direct contrast to the existing grandstand, and the use of the interrobang at the end of Ortega's question implies that anyone who disagrees that this is a 'terrific improvement' is obviously wrong. The use of light and open spaces in the second image juxtaposes tellingly with the first, seeking to further convince the audience of the clear choice in this binary opposition.

Ortega's language surrounding the proposal continues to be positive and community-minded towards the end of her speech. She refers to the contract between her firm and Goodgreens Developers as a 'partnership' and uses words such as 'revitalise' and 'rejuvenate' to describe the positive impact on the community, thereby seeking to evoke similarly positive associations in the minds of her audience. Harking back to the 'bustling, exciting Westhaven Shows many decades ago', Ortega suggests that the project will even have a nostalgic, traditional component that would resonate with older members of the audience, which indicates to these particular members that they haven't been overlooked in the planning of the development. Ortega also mentions the benefits to the public, including a 'club restaurant', 'purpose-built public running track' and 'beautiful, well-kept parklands'. Briefly mentioning the 'much-needed tourist dollars', Ortega covers all her bases, from economic to emotional considerations, ensuring that her audience is presented with a variety of arguments that may sway them to approve of the proposed development.

Ortega ends her speech by reassuring her audience that this venture will result not in the loss of a public space, but in the beginning of a 'whole new world' of opportunities for the town. The landscape architect stresses the openness of the development plans and invites listeners to stay and ask her any questions about the proposal. The use of an approachable and understanding tone here stresses to the audience that this is a collaborative endeavour, making them feel that their voices will be heard. Assuming their support in the final sentence, Ortega signs off by stating that she 'look[s] forward' to seeing her listeners 'on the greens', a strong proclamation that leaves the audience with the positive and confident impression that Ortega has progressively built throughout her speech.

Sample response 10: Fast fashion

Opening with a rhetorical question ('Does the person in this cartoon look familiar?'), Alessandra DuBois of Alessandra's Thrifty Chic Store begins her post, 'Fast fashion? Let's slow it down', with a direct address to her readers – many of whom are already followers of her store's social media accounts – asking them to connect with the post's issues. Her second sentence identifies the topic: the thoughtless consumption of 'fast fashion', embodied by 'someone who buys on-trend outfits … without taking the time to consider the ramifications of their shopping habits'. In a concerned, informative and rational tone, DuBois' first paragraph sets the mood for the rest of the piece, and is intended to immediately emphasise to her readers why they should join her fight against fast fashion and its negative impacts on individuals, communities and the environment. However, in order to ensure that she does not intimidate her audience with too stern an opening, she includes in her second paragraph acknowledgement that people might not even be aware that they are part of the problem. She hopes that making her readers aware that fast fashion is a significant issue will encourage them to modify their own behaviour and even try to influence others; as noted at the beginning of the piece, the blog is intended as an 'intervention' for those who are supporting fast fashion. The choice of the word 'intervention' – emphasised with bold text – lends weight to her argument, as its connotations link the issue to serious behavioural problems such as drug addiction. By imploring readers to help *others* transform their behaviour, the blog is likely to make the reader feel motivated and virtuous about contributing to positive change.

Having engaged her audience at a personal level, DuBois shifts her focus to support her argument with firm evidence: facts and figures gleaned from relevant organisations and publications (such as TRAID and *The Ethical Consumer*). She cites more than one source, and the cumulation of evidence showing the harmful impact of fast fashion serves to emphasise the significance and scale of the issue. Including authoritative and impactful statistics allows DuBois to demonstrate that her assertions are reliable and fact-based, pre-empting potential criticism that her argument is purely subjective. The use of numerical data also enables her to continue the instructive tone established previously, and to present herself as trustworthy and compassionate in seeking to empower her readers with knowledge. Though there is a strong focus on statistics, DuBois balances this section with emotive language to ensure that it keeps readers engaged and does not become too dry. Words and phrases such as 'toxic culture that harms', 'exploits', 'scare' and 'urgency' contribute to a mounting sense of catastrophe, moving readers to wish to take action to prevent such an outcome.

In the sixth paragraph, there is a significant shift away from the use of statistical, concrete evidence. Here, DuBois employs a familiar pop-culture reference to 'fashion horror flick, *The Devil Wears Prada*', to demonstrate her relatability and draw the issue back to 'the human element'. This humanisation underlies the second half of the post, in which DuBois places the emphasis on the individual, and on the ways in which each person might be able to help transform the terrible situation she has brought to readers' attention. Linking this section back to earlier parts of the post, emotive language choices such as 'extremely hazardous', 'terribly low pay' and 'sweatshops and child labour are rife' are used to create images that are both alarming and hard to dismiss, priming the reader to want to be part of the solution, or the 'simple fix'.

In the post's second significant shift in tone – prompted by a rhetorical question ('how can anyone consciously continue to support fast fashion?'), echoing the opening sentence – DuBois discloses a very personal interest in the subject: she has a financial investment in combating fast fashion. The positioning of this revelation within the argument is careful. Rather than including it early, which could make the post seem self-promoting, she first positions herself as someone passionate about the issue, then explains that her business offers a way forward, in stopping 'the vicious cycle of wastage'. Thus she hopes to achieve two goals: to change perceptions and behaviour regarding fashion, and also to benefit personally from this when customers buy from her shop instead of relying on fast fashion. (It should also be noted that readers of her blog are likely to be aware of her shop, so she expects them to show some customer loyalty.)

An image at this point contributes to the inspiring mood DuBois is attempting to create. Just as the text now offers an optimistic alternative to the doom and gloom detailed in the first half, so this image contrasts with the cartoon at the start of the post. The cartoon's monochrome tones contribute to the dramatic contrast between the woman – well-dressed, with the shape and posture of a catwalk model, and carrying enough bags to suggest that she is somewhat reckless in her shopping – and the scene she is walking away from. Behind, near a digger at a tip, a tied-up rubbish bag contrasts with the woman's pristine shopping bags, symbolising the direct transition from fashion to waste. The image presents a world in which the impact of fast fashion is inevitable and destructive, and nobody bothers to give it a second thought (suggested by the woman looking firmly ahead, not behind). The second image, however, reinforces the concept of 'slow fashion', which DuBois endorses, and uses a much gentler greyscale palette. As a photograph rather than a cartoon, the image suggests that this new alternative is real and concrete. The positive words on the tag – 'care', 'respect', 'fair' – suggest that positive change, too, can be real, while the phrase 'sustainable fashion' provides a substitute for 'fast fashion', and readers are encouraged to link this alternative to DuBois' shop. By the end of the post, the phrase she uses is 'slow fashion', highlighting the post's structural progression from problem to solution and encouraging readers to make a similar progression in their responses to the post, from feelings of alarm to feelings of hope.

In the final paragraphs, DuBois continues with her sense of optimism about the future of fashion, providing numerous examples of ways that readers can shift behaviour and avert ultimate disaster. Key terms include 'sustainably', 'durable', 'natural' and 'eco-friendly', and the positive connotations of this new vocabulary support her assertion that, if we make these choices, 'we would have collectively made a sizeable difference in bringing fast fashion to a screeching halt'. At this stage there is a change from the earlier frequent use of the second person 'you', which has made readers feel personally responsible, to the inclusive 'we', which is likely to make them more inclined to accept suggestions of how they might contribute to a solution. She now welcomes the reader into a community of people who are doing the right thing, and who are powerful enough to improve 'the very future of our planet'. This concluding paragraph offers an uplifting prompt to go forth and enact positive change.

Sample response 11: Sunflower plantations

The residents of Sunnyside, a small regional town known for its sunflower plantations, are struggling to deal with the influx of tourists seeking photos of the crops in bloom. The local farmers are particularly concerned that the visitors are damaging the sunflowers. Harvey Sunshine, one such local farmer, is addressing a group of locals and council members to present his proposed solution to the issue – charge visitors a small fee for accessing the fields. A photo of Sunshine inspecting his sunflower crop is also on display during the delivery of his speech.

Sunshine's speech to an audience of locals and town councillors opens with a self-deprecating tone. He acknowledges his reputation as the 'resident curmudgeon', but goes on to present this as a desirable quality because it allows him to speak up about important issues when necessary. He does not immediately identify the focus of his speech; instead, he works to overcome the initial resistance he appears to expect from his listeners. The farmer anticipates the possibility that his audience will dismiss him due to his reputation, and he states that 'every now and then, axes need grinding'. This positive refashioning of the somewhat dismissive phrase 'constant axe to grind' encourages the audience to focus on the issue rather than on the personality of the speaker. Sunshine further engages the audience through his use of inclusive language, referring to 'our beloved community' and 'my fellow farmers'. In doing so he elevates the issue beyond a personal grievance, and suggests he is discussing something of concern to all residents of Sunnyside, positioning the audience to feel that he and they are on the same side in this debate.

While Sunshine acknowledges that 'tourists have always been a presence at Sunnyside', his use of emotive terms such as 'hordes … armed to the teeth' and 'belligerents' encourages the audience to regard the current 'huge increase' in tourism as a threat. The focus on the negative aspects of the visitors positions the audience to agree that the tourists are a problem for the Sunnyside farmers. Sunshine concludes his criticism of the tourists by voicing the question he has led the audience to ponder – 'what's to be done?' Having identified the number of tourists as a problem, this question aims to focus his listeners' attention on finding a solution.

Sunshine condemns the local council's suggestion that there is 'nothing we can do' as 'absolute cowardice', and it is contrasted starkly with his call for 'urgent and concerted action'. The audience is likely to share Sunshine's view, having been positioned to regard the tourists as a threat that must be addressed. His use of the phrase 'they tell us' imposes a divide between the council and the rest of the Sunnyside population, encouraging the audience to reject the council's position and thus become more receptive to Sunshine's ideas. This desire for action is further enhanced by Sunshine's fear-inducing statement that something must be done 'if sunflowers are to have any kind of future here in our community'. This creates a sense of urgency, as the sunflower industry is important to the local economy. The sunflower is 'a very fragile plant'; his claim that he has personally seen tourists 'trample hundreds of dollars underfoot' and 'snap the heads off' the sunflowers reminds listeners that this is a significant problem. The image adds to this argument, showing Sunshine inspecting the damage done to his flowers. The apparently candid shot presents sunflower farming in practical terms, showing it to be a crop needing attention and care, not just a tourist attraction or a photo opportunity. At the same time, the gentle way in which Sunshine is touching the flowers testifies to his care for them, reminding viewers that these flowers have a greater significance to the town in terms of their beauty and the positive reputation this gives Sunnyside.

Moreover, Sunshine links the vulnerable state of the sunflower crops with that of the farmers of Sunnyside, suggesting that, like him, many are at the point of considering leaving the town or giving up sunflower cultivation due to the 'crisis' of overtourism. This appeal to the audience's sympathy builds on earlier descriptions of his animals being stressed and his grandchildren restricted in their play due to inconsiderate visitors, creating an impression of an area under siege and positioning the audience to want to act to protect both Sunshine and farmers generally.

Sunshine's proposed solution is presented in an enthusiastic tone. He introduces it by stating that it is 'simple', suggesting that the problem can be addressed with little effort. His use of positive words, such as 'boon', 'benefit', 'opportunities' and a 'potential' that is 'limitless', work to make his proposal appealing to his audience. Sunshine's final call to action appeals to his audience's desire to protect and support their local community, implying that if they do not act the whole town will suffer.

Harvey Sunshine's speech is a conservative appeal to his local community, encouraging them to support a plan to reduce the negative impacts of tourism in their town.

Sample response 12: Video games in the English classroom

Speaking at a state conference, experienced English teacher Margaret Lee presents a passionate argument encouraging teachers to adopt video games as a legitimate form of text. Appealing to her audience's concern for their students' development, Lee argues that video games are not only a valid and engaging text type; they also offer students who struggle with literacy an engaging way into narrative texts. Throughout her presentation Lee speaks of the modern advances in video games, using images to underline her main points and emphasising her own teaching experience as a way of offering empathetic understanding to teachers who may be reluctant to use video games as study texts.

Lee begins by establishing video games as a modern and exciting opportunity for students, arguing that the format has evolved over time, beyond typical negative perceptions. Opening with a heartfelt 'thank you' to her 'fellow English teachers', Lee aims to establish a rapport with her potentially reluctant audience. She readily acknowledges that many teachers 'might never have thought' of games as learning tools but appeals to a sense of modernity through the words and phrases 'new opportunity', 'exciting' and 'modern universe'. Lee also uses the tricolon 'to learn, to analyse and to study' to emphasise that games are not just for entertainment but in fact have academic applications. Aware that her audience is likely unfamiliar with these applications, she states that some 'might even believe that video games lead to aggression', the 'even' in that sentence serving to highlight the apparent absurdity of the belief, thus positioning her audience to want to distance themselves from it.

Lee's argument shifts focus to account for some of these negative perceptions of video games, and to offer her opinion on the academic benefits. The image that serves as a backdrop for this part of her speech – an expansive open world with a lone horse and rider – is a far cry from the 'violent, repetitive games' and 'days of punching sticky buttons' that may be the stereotypes associated with gaming. This loaded language, with its antisocial connotations, develops a dichotomy between outdated understandings of video games and the new style of game she promotes, which the audience is encouraged to feel excited about. Lee claims that the games she is proposing for the classroom are 'more sophisticated', selecting her words carefully to appeal to this experienced and knowledgeable audience. She normalises using games as texts, comparing video games with the films that experienced teachers are 'so used to analysing'. The first image supports this, with the horserider at the top of a hill surveying a vast natural expanse, suggesting new worlds to be explored. The use of natural imagery helps to present video games as healthy and stimulating, while the detail and realism of the picture emulates a film, the already commonly studied text type that Lee likens video games to, encouraging the audience to view video games as equally 'rich' and worthy texts.

Lee also uses vocabulary that the English-teaching audience would be familiar with, targeting typical text features such as 'narrative structure', 'historical context' and 'genre' to address concerns that video games are meant for entertainment rather than study. Video games that present 'historically accurate worlds', Lee argues, also give students an 'advantage' in their learning. She cites the findings of studies by 'cognitive scientists' to further support her argument as to the benefits of video games, including improving specific skills such as 'decision-making' and 'coordination' that go beyond those developed through reading the traditional novel text type. Drawing on expert evidence in this way is intended to reassure the audience that her opinion is based on research and that her claims can be relied on.

Continuing to address the potential reluctance of her audience, Lee empathises with teachers who may struggle with the concept of games as text, but highlights the value to students. Her informal and frank admission when she states, 'I won't lie to you – I hated the idea' of introducing games, is intended to build a sense of shared concern with her audience and encourages them to share her journey of discovery with regard to the benefits of video games. She targets valid concerns such as students losing the 'only … opportunity' to study classics if novels, plays and poems are removed from the curriculum. However, Lee then projects an image of happy, engaged students using a tablet, to underscore her counterpoint: the interests of the students should be put ahead of the interests of the teacher. The students in the image are laughing and apparently engaged in what they are viewing; their physical closeness suggests collaboration and teamwork. The attractive classroom background evokes a stimulating, modern learning environment, reinforcing the idea of video games as important elements in the future of English studies. Lee punctuates her presentation at this point with a short sentence aimed at emphasising a fundamental point: 'Then I considered my students'. The implication is that a teacher who remains inflexible on text choices is inconsiderate, whereas a teacher who can 'put aside [their] own preferences' is more focused on helping students, a position her audience of educated teachers is likely to want to identify with. The empathetic nature of her argument shifts from teachers to students, as Lee encourages the audience to think of the 'struggling' students who find it 'arduous' to read a whole novel, emotive language with connotations of physical labour and exhaustion that draw on the audience's natural sympathy for their students and concern for their welfare. Her final question even suggests that students might feel 'more confident' about picking up a novel once they have developed the skills to 'analyse and interpret' through video games, a suggestion that draws on the shared desire of her audience to see their students embrace English studies.

In closing, Lee reiterates her empathetic stance that she 'understand[s]' some in the audience may be 'feeling reluctant' to introduce video games, an approach she depends on throughout the presentation in order to present herself as relatable and informed about the challenges faced by English teachers. Ultimately, however, Lee ends on a positivc call to action, challenging English teachers to explore the 'rich texts' of video games.

Sample response 13: Keeping cats indoors

Appearing on the research-based news and analysis website *The Conversation*, the article 'One cat, one year, 110 native animals …' brings together research from 66 different studies to support the argument that pet cats should be kept indoors at all times in order to protect native wildlife. While the article was written by a team of academics and professors, the use of accessible language throughout is intended to reach a broad readership, with the key target audience being cat owners, and particularly those who allow their pets to roam outdoors.

Unsurprisingly for an article with an academic context, the piece relies heavily on statistics, data and research findings. Sobering figures are introduced throughout, such as 'each roaming pet cat kills 186 reptiles, birds and mammals per year, most of them native to Australia'. This underscores the reliability and specialist knowledge of the writers, encouraging readers to accept the writers' opinions as well-informed and supported by other experts on the subject matter. While the heavy use of facts and figures helps to make their argument appear objective, the writers are not dispassionate or detached; their tone is firm and uncompromising throughout. Indeed, recognising that an onslaught of data can be dry, this information is frequently supplemented with evocative language to keep readers engaged. Use of emotive phrases such as 'wreaking havoc', 'the results are staggering', 'extraordinary level of predation' and, in the article title, 'killing machine' underscores the scale and urgency of the problem, priming the reader to take action.

The structure of the piece conforms to appropriate conventions for a research-based article, using subheadings to guide the reader, and laying the argument out logically. The first paragraph, for example, broadly outlines the issue, with the first sentence relying on inclusive language and the assumed shared knowledge that feral cats have long been acknowledged as pests. While readers may be reluctant to view their own pet as a 'killing machine', the writers here anticipate little resistance to the idea that cats in the wild pose a risk to wildlife. This uncontroversial opening therefore allows the writers to make a deft segue into their main argument – 'pet cats are wreaking havoc too' – without prompting defensiveness from the reader.

The following subheadings ('Surely not my cat' and 'Urban cats') then work to undermine any cognitive dissonance that would allow readers to accept feral cats as a risk to wildlife while refuting the same charge against domestic cats. The 'Urban cats' section, for example, encourages readers to reassess their way of thinking by pointing out that different roaming areas and densities mean that 'per square kilometre per year, pet cats kill 30–50 times more animals than feral cats in the bush'. Likewise, 'Surely not my cat' anticipates and contests the potential counterargument from cat owners that their pets do not hunt. These strategies are supported by the image accompanying the piece, showing a cat with its paw pressed against the lifeless form of a bird. As the cat appears clean and well taken care of, we can assume this is a domestic cat. The light colour of the bird indicates it is not one of the common feral bird species, so it could be rare or native, and its size underscores its vulnerability and evokes sympathy from the reader. This is supported by the use of phrases such as 'roam and hunt' to undermine the perception of domestic cats as harmless, repositioning them as predators.

Having presented an array of data and statistics that align pet cats with their feral equivalents, and having pre-empted potential counterarguments from pet owners, the writers put forth the only logical solution for anyone who owns a cat: 'keep it inside'. By referring to those who do this already as 'responsible pet owners', the writers do not need to directly call out owners of the '2.7 million pet cats – 71% of all pet cats – [who] are able to roam and hunt'. The implicit meaning is clear:

these owners are irresponsible. This jab works to create a sense of guilt for any readers who own cats and currently do not keep them contained. This is supported by the inclusive phrasing 'most of us want to see native wildlife around towns and cities', which appeals to readers' sense of community. Likewise, a later appeal to patriotism – 'compared to many other countries, the Australian public are more aware of how cats threaten native wildlife' – positions Australians as uniquely attuned to the dangers posed to our wildlife and suggests we are a population with an interest in environmental conservation. These appeals work together to create an image of Australians as united, both in a wider sociopolitical sense and on a more micro neighbourhood level. To disagree with the argument put forward would then place pet owners in opposition to the broader goals and interests of their community.

However, the writers appear to acknowledge that there is little point appealing to pet owners' sense of guilt without offering a solution. The section under the subheading 'What can pet owners do?' reiterates the writers' contention that 24-hour containment is the only option available to cat owners, and again the writers anticipate and rebut potential counterarguments. While placing a bell on a cat's collar may reduce its effectiveness as a hunter, the only way to prevent hunting completely is to keep it inside. The evidence presented thus far may be enough to convince non-pet-owning readers. But to ensure they are reaching those cat owners who may feel uncomfortable keeping their pets indoors, the writers include a final appeal focusing on the benefits of containment for cats themselves: it protects them from injury and 'unwanted breeding'; it prevents them from fighting with other cats; and it prevents the spread of disease. The writers end their piece with a strong appeal to the interests of cat owners resistant to indoor lifestyles for their pets: the primary target audience of this article and potentially the hardest to reach. The article concludes with an acknowledgement that to keep one's pets indoors may be challenging, but, again, that not doing so is irresponsible.

Emphasising their reliability as experts in the field, the writers compile a vast array of evidence to support their contention that cats must be kept inside to protect local ecosystems. These figures and statistical evidence are supplemented with powerful, evocative phrases and various emotional appeals that seek to reposition domestic cats in the minds of readers as predators rather than just pets. Combining these approaches, the article appeals directly to pet owners who do not currently keep their cats contained – the key demographic who can make a difference to this issue.

Sample response 14: Tax on red meat

Concerned about the health and environmental harms of red meat production and consumption, columnist Parminder Preciosa argues in her opinion piece that red meat should be taxed.

From its outset, Parminder Preciosa's article adopts a friendly tone. The alliterative heading, 'Taxing the T-bone', and the idiomatic subheading, 'it's time to give red meat the chop', humorously encapsulate her contention that a healthier, more ethical (albeit costlier) approach to red meat consumption is necessary for the sake of the individual, the economy and the environment. Preciosa's opening argument is an anecdote concerning the perils of passive smoking, to pique her audience's curiosity about possible negative connections between red meat and cigarettes. The writer imagines a diner being subjected to a sensory assault by insensitive smokers, an allusion to the laws around 'smoking in the twenty-first century' to which her adult readers can easily relate. This, coupled with her repeated use of personal pronouns ('you', 'your' and 'yourself') and the bombardment of negative present continuous verbs ('stinging … clinging … poisoning'), immerses the reader in a toxic environment and positions them to feel fearful, frustrated and incensed at the dangers and disrespect they and others in the community face.

This is reinforced by the accompanying visual of a plate of meat sculpted into the shape of a question mark, a vivid image that serves to provokes readers' further cautious curiosity about this issue. The meat is raw, which is likely to arouse readers' disgust. In the same way, its lone presence on the plate, with no accompaniments, makes it unlike any genuine meal, thus encouraging readers to reject the idea of eating red meat as distasteful and even unnatural. The stark lighting and unadorned place-setting reinforces the unappetising nature of the image.

Following her emotive and vivid opening, the writer shifts to a more dogmatic tone to educate about and warn against the 'elevated risk' to one's health from consuming carcinogenic meats, which Preciosa states is comparable to the risks of smoking. She supports her argument by citing the authoritative World Health Organization and alarming statistics regarding mortality rates and environmental damage caused by meat production; these imply a sense of danger in eating everyday consumables such as 'pepperoni pizza' and 'bacon', appealing to readers' fear for themselves and their families. These ordinary items are likely to be consumed by most readers, thus personalising the issue for them and reinforcing the idea that meat-eating is a direct threat to their wellbeing.

Drawing on testimony from a variety of respected sources, including scientific journals and the WHO, lends Preciosa's argument credence, suggesting that she has investigated the issue thoroughly before forming her conclusion. Moreover, citing several expert sources implies widespread agreement with her position, inclining readers to wish to position themselves among the majority rather than a dissenting minority.

Continuing in a more optimistic tone, the writer highlights again her proposal that a meat tax would serve both personal and community values. By juxtaposing the negative connotations of the 'threat' and 'enormous strain' associated with current untaxed meat consumption against the potential of 'positive … healthier' outcomes, Preciosa offers a logical alternative that positions community stakeholders to agree that such a tax would have a moral value, outweighing any monetary cost. Her shift to a more hopeful tone aims at encouraging the reader to think that there is a solution to the enormous problem she has outlined with meat consumption: a tax that would help to reduce consumption and offset the damage it causes.

Further, to widen her moral argument, the writer moves from local to global implications of meat production; she employs confronting language such as 'catastrophic … problem … worse … unethical … slaughter … kills' to conjure imagery of large-scale death and destruction that any reader would have difficulty condoning, arousing both their sympathy and their outrage. Concluding, Preciosa once again reins in her alarmist polemic and transitions back to her initial personable, measured tone, acknowledging the importance of individual choice while reiterating her appeal to the community's collective conscience regarding the dangers posed by red meat. This has the effect of reassuring any readers who might have been deterred by her strident tone that the substance of her argument is logical and ethical.

Appearing in the local newspaper with a broad general audience, Preciosa's opinion piece aims to mount several arguments in favour of a meat tax to appeal to different segments of this audience. Likewise, her reliance on both emotional appeals and scientific evidence caters to a wide cross-section of the populace. Her contention is bolstered by recurrent appeals to reader values of morality and fairness, claiming support for the community and the environment in fervent tones, and demanding engagement from local readers.

Sample response 15: Coffee pods

In 'What our love affair with coffee pods reveals about our values', posted on *The Conversation* website, John Rice and Nigel Martin contend in a scolding and sometimes mocking tone that our consumption of coffee pods and the glib promotional material associated with them tests our commitment to a sensible and sustainable approach to coffee consumption.

The article immediately establishes Rice's and Martin's credibility with the disclosure notice that identifies the former's affiliation with a political party and the latter's lack of vested interests, thus suggesting their transparency and honesty. Furthermore *The Conversation*'s emphasis on academic content encourages readers to believe that the writers' arguments and use of evidence are based on sound research and practices. Their purposeful use of alarming statistics and research that highlights '28 billion capsules' and '28 million kilograms of aluminium' contributing to landfill positions readers to view their research as detailed and sound. Coupled with the reference to and quotation from American satirist HL Mencken, the authors present themselves as educated authorities and invite readers to accept their stance on the 'march of the pods'.

To offset the risk of alienating the average reader by stamping their academic authority on the issue, Rice and Martin utilise inclusive language and promote accountability in 'Australian homes and workplaces'. Their consistent use of inclusive language in such phrases as 'many of us', 'we' and 'our love affair' firmly lays the burden of responsibility on all coffee consumers. Readers are urged to recognise themselves as belonging to the generalised groups of 'late sleepers', 'latte socialists', 'Western consumers' or even 'Australians' who have contributed to the 'problem in our society'. Having conceded such complicity, readers are likely to feel compelled to acknowledge their susceptibility to shrewd advertising and therefore to accept the writers' assertion that their own behaviour is partly to blame. The writers' scathing tone aids in the depiction of the unacceptable 'behemoth' multinational and its 'usurpers', who endorse the 'vices embodied in pods', as 'rapacious' and greedy. Yet, it is the consumers who are duped into accepting 'barely 5 grams' of 'watery, musty and underwhelming' coffee in 'blind taste tests'. The mocking tonal shift admonishes consumers simply 'wooed' by a 'Hollywood star' to indulge our 'love of convenience' or 'laziness'. A reprimand from Rice and Martin identifies readers' presumed 'pangs of guilt' as they 'conveniently' secrete pods into a 'collecting receptacle' for later disposal. The use of inclusive language and negative connotations lures readers into accepting responsibility for their uncritical acceptance of clever marketing and the resulting increase in pod numbers.

Rice and Martin use appeals to fear to paint a 'less than rosy picture for the future'. They evoke a sense of fear and anxiety in readers by announcing 'the news is far from all good' and conjuring images of disasters such as a 'tsunami' and the peril of an 'ageing Soviet nuclear power plant'. The prime threat is to sustainable living and environmental health, which are susceptible to 'problems' associated with bulging landfill sites. Not even the promise of 'recyclable' or 'vegetable-based biodegradable' capsules allays readers' fears as the relentless proliferation of 'aluminium or double-wrapped plastic pods' dumped in landfill negates any benefit from recycling. The clean and 'green' hopes of readers are diminished as the warning of supressed 'recycling figures' suggests that these negative statistics would be too 'egregious' to release. Readers are finally manipulated to fear the 'sourcing practices' of Nestlé, Nespresso, Aldi and Cafitally as they focus on 'self-serving' behaviours that deliver limited benefits to struggling 'third world' countries. Not only is environmental sustainability called into question but Rice and Martin firmly imply that readers should join in the growing criticism levelled at 'coffee pod innovators' for deliberately undermining and taking advantage of these besieged 'coffee-growing communities'.

Rice and Martin incorporate an image into their article – a photograph of innumerable used coffee pods amassed in a disordered heap. The implication for viewers and readers is that their 'love affair' with the pods ultimately leads to 'conveniently secreted' masses of packaging destined for the bin and eventually landfill. The number of pods implies the vastness of the problem, while the way in which they are discarded suggests carelessness and a lack of concern for the environment, positioning readers to feel both alarmed and critical. Like councils and local community leaders, viewers are positioned to consider how to dispose of this growing mound of used receptacles, significantly detracting from the 'positive haze' presented by marketers.

Ultimately, Rice and Martin utilise a range of persuasive techniques to convince readers that our voracious consumption of coffee is contributing to an ensuing environmental calamity, and they chastise consumers for their reluctance to 'do anything about it'. Their astute use of research and statistics, interspersed with a healthy 'cynical' approach to multinational coffee companies, cautions an educated audience regarding the dangers of blindly accepting the 'self-serving' claims of any industry. The integrated visual compels readers to acknowledge the sheer size of the problem and the smug indifference of corporate decision-makers. Furthermore, the authors' use of inclusive language and appeals encourages consumers, even the 'budget-conscious' seduced by the coffee pod, to resist participating in 'environmental profligacy'.

Sample response 16: Children and screen time

The surge of technological devices and their accessibility has resulted in an increase of computers, televisions, phones, tablets and interactive games in the home and school environment. Their popularity as a learning tool has prompted many parents and health professionals to voice their anxieties about the number of hours children spend in front of screens. In a letter in the weekly newsletter and addressed to the Wattletree school community, parent Asif Abdul claims, in a concerned tone, that parents need to monitor and manage their children's screen time for their health and wellbeing.

Abdul immediately establishes his identity as a parent of two school-aged boys, thereby confirming his credibility and authority to address the issue and informing his target audience of other concerned parents that he himself has fears and apprehensions. He openly invites the other parents to share in his views through the use of inclusive language, recognising their common qualms about 'our children' and how 'we need to be aware' of the obligations of parenthood. He also engages in a range of anecdotes offering more subtle appraisal of his own lack of vigilance monitoring screen time. He recounts the use of screens as a 'substitute babysitter', or to 'provide answers' or as 'a night-light', analysing possible motivations for increased screen time. His claim that these 'communication devices have become an integral part of parenting' is likely to be a familiar belief in many homes so parents reading the newsletter would easily acknowledge his point of view.

Once he has established a common link and shared experience with readers, Abdul cites Apple founder Steve Jobs and 'CEOs of tech companies' who have expressed 'similar ideas' about limiting their children's screen time. This has inspired him to follow the example set by the 'technological guru' and his suggestion is that readers should institute a similar plan. A range of experts – researchers from the American Academy of Pediatrics; neuroscientist Susan Greenfield; and Professor Gary Small – are also employed as authorities in their field who advocate that 'children learn best by interacting with people, not screens'. Readers are positioned to be impressed by the consensus of specialists and reassured that Adbul's viewpoint is shared by such a broad range of influential professionals, whose own conclusions are likely to be drawn from facts and evidence.

To support his assertions and engage parents further, Abdul employs appeals to fear, inciting additional parental alarm. He asserts that 'many reputable figures' and 'many doctors' warn of ensuing health, learning and social problems associated with extended screen time. Parents' fears for their children's health are manipulated by discussion of such potential damage as 'insidious' changes to 'people's brains' from internet use, the 'startling rate' of 'childhood obesity', 'eye strain', 'dehydration and sleep problems'. These threats, suggestive of wide-ranging and serious physical damage, aim to impress upon readers that Abdul's ideas and solutions are critical to maintaining the health and wellbeing of their vulnerable children.

Beyond impending health risks, parents are also pressured into accepting limits on screen time for social and educational reasons. The possibility that screen time will encourage 'little thought' and inhibit children's learning by fostering a 'shallow, superficial engagement with information' is intended to frighten and arouse the protective instincts of parents who want the best educational outcomes for their children. The additional concerns that children could be subject to 'cyberbullying' or exposed to inappropriate 'adult content' reinforces the need to adopt Abdul's recommendations immediately, to avoid further damage through extended hours in front of screens.

In his final paragraphs, Abdul's tone changes from concern to self-admonishment for his own lack of parenting skills. He outlines his dreams for his children to become 'informed, creative and imaginative adults'. His confessions of 'irresponsible' and 'quick-fix habits' to entertain children so he can finally 'enjoy a coffee' reveal his guilt over opting for screens to 'ward off boredom or fatigue or anger'. Readers have been positioned, through inclusive language and shared experience, to accept Abdul's research and statistical data as hard evidence for rejecting using screens in this way. Now they are urged to acknowledge their own failings alongside the writer and share in the only responsible way forward: '90 minutes' screen time a day', crayons and 'reading print books'. Abdul presumes that every parent holds the same dreams and hopes for their own children and by accepting his recommendations he hints that they will not only stave off future problems but gain a sense of satisfaction from their adept parenting.

The photograph incorporated into the letter depicts a young child entranced by a small phone screen and highlights many of Abdul's arguments. The child is situated in what looks like a public space in a school or library, with books sitting untouched on shelves in the background, literally left behind and dismissed. The viewer is positioned to observe the isolated child absorbed only with the screen and ignoring the potential diversions offered to engage young children in this learning environment. This encourages viewers to conclude, as Abdul has, that the ever-present lure of the screen continues to dominate children's choices, time and preferences, insulating them from the creative and interactive environments around them.

Excessive exposure to screens is promoting a number of health, social and educational problems in young children. Asif Abdul encourages readers to consider the detrimental impact of increased screen time on young and developing minds. His suggestions to limit screen time are supported with statistical evidence as well as references to experts and specialists from the medical and business sectors. His arguments are also illustrated strongly by the inclusion of an alarming image, while his use of inclusive language and anecdotal evidence identifies a target audience of concerned parents who share his desire to provide the best opportunities for their children. His solutions to the problems aim to help parents to promote healthy learning environments beyond the ubiquitous screens.

Sample response 17: Overtourism

Published in *The Australian Financial Review*, Fiona Carruthers' opinion piece adopts a highly personal tone to reflect on the problem of overtourism and who should be considered responsible for it. The author begins the article with a humorous anecdote that serves to establish her own stake in the issue. Recalling a recent trip to Tasmania, Carruthers recounts the events that led her to realise that she was a part of 'the problem' of overtourism – yet another traveller seeking out the latest hotspot and 'cluttering up the landscape' – rather than simply an observer. Throughout the anecdote Carruthers presents a satirical, tongue-in-cheek picture of the typical Western tourist, describing herself and her 'well-travelled' group of friends drinking white wine on a hike, crying into their 'rye three-seed crackers' and engaging in debates about the best times to travel to Rome or Lisbon. This self-deprecation is aimed at getting the reader onside and establishing a likeable and trustworthy persona that will incline them to believe her.

But as well as making fun of herself, she is also taking a veiled swipe at her readers. This is evident in the use of cues such as the reference to Patagonia (a well-known, but expensive, eco-wear brand) as well as the keep cup, both of which will be instantly recognisable to *The Australian Financial Review*'s readership, a typically middle- to upper-class well-educated audience. Instead of directly criticising the reader, however, Carruthers chooses to target herself and her friends as the objects of humour and derision. This strategy helps to keep the audience onside, encouraging them to interrogate their own complicity in the problems of overtourism without explicitly blaming them for their involvement.

In the next section, 'Slowing the tide', the author examines the issue of overtoursim in a broader context. With connotations of inevitability and futility, the reference to a rising tide builds on the imagery conjured in earlier paragraphs of tourist 'creep', in order to elicit a sense of foreboding in the reader. This is supported by the visual of a crowded beach, inundated with tourists to the point of saturation, as well as the previous reference to travellers 'climbing all over' the Sydney Harbour Bridge – both of which work to add to a sense of an impending threat.

Despite this, however, Carruthers' tone remains deliberately playful and facetious. She acknowledges the UNWTO's argument that a solution 'must be forged by residents and tourists', accepting its logic – 'a good point when you consider that most of us fit both descriptions at some point' – and she subtly mocks the impulse to blame the usual suspects for the problem ('social media, the gig economy and low-cost travel providers'). The introduction of the pronouns 'us' and 'we' also marks a development in the author's argumentative strategy, from allowing readers to draw parallels between the author's experience as a tourist and the wider problem, to expressly including readers in the problem. The 'we' used in 'we also like to blame social media', for example, is a reminder that the audience is just as much a part of overtourism as the author is.

Broadening the scope of her argument to examine a historical perspective, Carruthers goes on to expand her target beyond herself and the reader to include the entire human race, tracing the issue of overtourism to accounts from ancient Greece to the early twentieth century. Adopting a more didactic tone, she uses references to historical figures such as Pausanias and Marco Polo to bolster the persuasiveness of her argument and employs a descriptive quote from EM Forster to illustrate some of the uncanny similarities between tourism in the twentieth and the twenty-first centuries.

But Carruthers never strays too far from her ironic, tongue-in-cheek delivery. The imagery of cavemen swapping their caves for ones with 'better views', or tourists returning home with counterfeit goods in the form of a fake Louis Vuitton purse, for example, encourages the audience to laugh at themselves; and the personal addresses to the reader ('Sound familiar?') reinforce the sense that the reader is both in on the joke and also the subject of it. The light and humorous tone also works to soften the impact of some of the more serious points, including the conclusions of the Tourism Recreation Research think tank, for example, which 'groans' that mass tourism has been a characteristic of human nature for centuries.

After exploring the wider context of the problem, Carruthers pivots to examine solutions to the overtourism 'scourge', turning her attention to the 'staycation'. The use of portmanteau here, in the fusing of 'stay' and 'vacation', is another nod to the intended audience – a group of largely well-educated middle-class readers with a disposable income – and another tongue-in-cheek jibe at the tourism industry. After reporting the opinion of her well-travelled colleague, however, Carruthers comes full circle – knowingly falling into the same trap she found herself in at the beginning of the article and searching for the next big (albeit local) tourist destination. Employing her particular brand of self-deprecation, the author admits that, while she might 'publicly lament overtourism', she is still driven by the need to 'get in ahead of the pack'. As she sees it, the problem is too entrenched to solve – because 'that's what us humans do'.

But the effect of the ending isn't entirely negative. Again employing her strategy of holding herself up as the object of mirth, Carruthers leaves readers to decide if they will be content to follow her lead and continue to participate in the issue of overtourism, or if they will instead take steps to change their behaviour.

Sample response 18: Mobile phones and jaywalking

Wendy Squires has composed an informal opinion piece warning against the personal and societal dangers of mobile phone use by pedestrians, as well as discussing the challenge jaywalking poses to the safety of others. Those directly addressed – the 'wexters', lawmakers and enforcers, as well as 'the rest of us', members of the broader community – are informed of this menace by the writer's highly personalised polemic. Squires adopts a vehement tone to condemn pedestrians who ignore traffic and traffic signals while on their phones, outlining the physical risks, legal consequences and bleak future landscape we can expect if the problem continues, while also offering positive alternative pursuits to appeal to her readership's collective conscience.

From the outset, Squire's article deploys an exasperated tone. The alarming title, which ties mobile phone use to the negative and frightening imagery of 'zombie' and 'plague', creates the impression of a life-threatening disease affecting the entire population. The phrase 'completely out of control' adds a sense of disarray and excess to the picture. Together, these language choices act to support the author's clear contention that the distraction caused by mobile phone use has reached epidemic levels, and that change is needed for the benefit of our individual and collective wellbeing.

The writer's first argument focuses on the insensitivity and disrespectfulness of pedestrians 'transfixed' by their mobile phones. The use of colloquial language in the opening anecdote – including phrases such as 'easy tenner', 'young guy', 'ten bucks' and 'my mate' – reflects both the writer's humanity and relatability, and the casual, regular incidence of such hazardous behaviour. This is underscored by the busy image, showing several people in close proximity adopting the same narrow-visioned, narrow-minded pose (hunched over their phones, without awareness of the world around them). These written and visual cues compel the reader to empathise with Squires when she wishes she 'had lost the bet', and encourage the audience to draw a connection between the ignorance of mobile phone users and the unsettling sense of entitlement affecting our society.

Squires goes on to expand her attack by discussing the legal status of jaywalking, as well as the physical dangers such behaviours represent – not only for the 'wexters' themselves, but also for those around them. She employs historical allusion to draw mocking parallels between the widely denounced 'jaywalkers' of bygone years – renowned for their stupidity and ignorance – and contemporary mobile-phone-obsessed pedestrians, the latter being lawbreakers responsible for an upsurge in road deaths around the world. By weaving these broader repercussions together with her own 'near brush' experiences with jaywalking 'zombies', Squires presents an impression of a society in chaos. This positions readers to feel anger at the avoidable, senseless loss arising from such behaviours, something any safety-conscious individual would wish to distance themselves from.

Transitioning to a more frustrated and frank tone, Squires shifts from the micro- to the macro-perspective and outlines some of the measures that have been put into place to address the issue of accidents caused by 'ignorant and self-immersed' mobile phone users. Squires illustrates her argument by listing evidence of some of the more sophisticated techniques employed by cities to tackle the problem – from the 'Virtual Crash Billboard' in Paris, to in-ground lights in Melbourne and Sydney and spray machines in China. This is infused with a sense of escalating fear, generated by the use of words like 'deaths … injuries … danger … screeching' and 'terror' and the repetitive drilling of the urgent 'needs'. Together, these elements are designed to appeal to the readers' sense of safety, superiority and common sense, and spark outrage against the superficial, selfish and senseless 'wexters' who place water damage to their phones above personal safety.

Concluding her piece, Squires adopts an adamant tone (as evidenced in the unequivocal phrase, 'I refuse to apologise') to confirm her position as a virtuous commentator. The collection of positive descriptors (such as 'lucky', 'happily' and 'carefree'), together with the reference to activities such as walking her dog ('contemplation and exercise'), communicate the writer's sense of individuality, mental liberty and clarity. This is juxtaposed against the 'white noise' worshipped by the 'jays' referenced in the final paragraph. Dismissing mobile phone users in this way creates a 'them-against-us' perspective, intended to manipulate readers' desire for exclusivity and superiority, encouraging them to align with the author's position by moderating their mobile phone use and focusing on the here and now.

Squires' opinion piece is a passionate call for action on the issue of incessant distraction that stems from constant mobile phone use, which ultimately endangers the individual and those around them. Appealing to the reader's sense of morality and fairness, Squires demands engagement from those who value safety on the roads as well as their own physical and emotional wellbeing.

Sample response 19: Giving gifts, not things

Concerned about 'consumerism gone mad', Athena, a young professional woman, has decided to take a different approach to choosing Christmas gifts. She gives an informal speech to her family when they gather for their Christmas meal, handing out personalised cards to each person while she speaks. Each card includes a flyer for one of Athena's 'favourite charities', which advocates making a donation as a form of gift giving. Athena explains in a humorous and passionate tone why she has decided she won't be 'buying stuff for presents anymore', and earnestly seeks to convince her family to agree that her approach to gifts is both more meaningful and less wasteful than traditional gift-giving.

Athena begins by addressing her audience directly and in some cases individually. She acknowledges how much she loves Christmas and refers to her family's Christmas traditions, including her father's custard and 'the traditional Lee family lawn bowls tournament'. This establishes a warm and affectionate connection with her audience and clarifies that her break from the tradition of buying gifts is not a rejection of Christmas or all its traditions. Instead, she presents it as entirely in keeping with the 'time of giving', a familiar expression that all her family will know and relate to, and as part of her search to find 'better ways to show … love'. In this way she aims to reassure her family and overcome any initial resistance to her ideas or potential disappointment they may feel.

As she continues, Athena emphasises the positive aspects of the gifts she has chosen, encouraging her audience to see these as no less caring or beneficial than conventional presents. She outlines the various alternative gifts she has chosen, focusing on the care and thought that she put into each one. Her 'experience gifts' and 'IOU vouchers' are tailored to each recipient, and she demonstrates this by highlighting some of her choices – a 'high tea' for her grandmother, 'weeding the garden' for her mother and sewing for the twins. Moreover, Athena explains the ways in which these gifts offer various sources of pleasure and enjoyment, just as conventional presents do, again forestalling any reservations in her audience. Athena's gifts that take the form of 'contributions … to a bunch of different charities' are less obviously sources of pleasure for their recipients, so she describes these using positive expressions such as 'you will love knowing' to suggest these, too, will bring happiness to her family members, as well as to those who will benefit more directly from the donation.

Having reassured her audience that she has still provided meaningful gifts for each person, Athena goes on to reinforce the advantages of these gifts – particularly the donations – through an ethical argument, using words such as 'responsibility' and 'duty' just as she had used words such as 'fun stuff' and 'happy' in the first part of her speech. She asks her family to recognise that they 'have a responsibility to understand our privilege' and share their 'financial and social wealth', appealing to their sense of community and obligation, as well as their power to do good. In this way she combines the happiness attached to gift giving and receiving with a sense of ethical or moral duty. She repeats the inclusive 'we' – 'we have plenty of food, we have jobs, we have homes' – creating a sense of shared privilege, encouraging all her family members to feel that they too should consider presents within a wider social context, and making Athena's actions seem less extreme or peculiar.

The wider benefits of making a donation as a gift are also conveyed by the flyer for Level Up. The text within the flyer suggests that a donation 'really matters' and will help build 'a better world for all of us', reinforcing the ethical appeals in Athena's speech. The visual language adds to the positive messaging, through images of hearts, hands being raised, and the repetition of 'help' in large capitals. The flourishing tree full of hands and gently rolling hills create a peaceful feeling, building on the idea of 'helping hands' solving problems; some of these problems are identified in much smaller text, suggesting that these issues, though serious, can be overcome through positive action. The varied shades of the hands also convey the idea of an inclusive, diverse community that can be fostered through ethical gift giving. The overall impression is that a calmer and more caring world 'for all of us' can be created.

In the central part of her argument Athena moves on from her positive messages about community and helping others to strongly question the morality of consumerism as well as the waste associated with having 'THINGS' and 'STUFF'; the emphasis on these words, indicated by capital letters, reinforces the sense of excess and even greed she attaches to material possessions. She passionately asks her audience to consider the bigger social issues of 'environmental costs', 'ethical sustainability' and the 'treatment of workers'. She addresses her family's potential rejoinder that they are 'supporting local small business' by reminding them that this too has a cost in terms of both money and time. She then reiterates her central point that she is 'not buying stuff for presents anymore'. This negative representation of gift buying – characterised by 'wasting', 'panicking' and 'ridiculously high fees' – positions her audience to think critically about their own actions and to question behaviour that might have seemed normal or even virtuous, making them more receptive to Athena's own approach.

Once Athena establishes the reasons for her decision, she explains to her family how they can also benefit. She points out that they do not need to 'pretend' to appreciate her gifts, and gives examples of situations where gifts can sometimes miss the mark. This return to a humorous tone diffuses the defensive tension that her audience may be feeling, demonstrating her understanding that her attack on consumerism could be taken as a criticism of her family's decision to buy Christmas gifts.

Athena's tone is scathing when she discusses consumer culture in the central part of her speech, but she frames this with a happy, confident and often humorous tone at the start and at the end, recognising that her family might find it difficult to accept her 'choice for this year'. She concludes by inviting her audience to 'get the lawn bowls going!', effectively bringing the focus back to the 'traditional' aspects of the day, with which she also began her speech, reassuring her family that she does not wish to do away with Christmas traditions altogether. By reminding her family of the important aspects of the Christmas celebration, she provides some perspective, positioning them to acknowledge their privilege and recognise the value of finding new and more meaningful ways to share their good fortune.

Sample response 20: Beach lessons

In 'Beach lessons', Zan Smith argues that young children need plenty of outdoor physical activity and that increasing the amount of screen time they have each day will only be harmful, both to their physical health and their overall mental development. Smith presents a balanced, reasoned view, framing her piece with her experiences with her own children, while also including evidence and guidelines from Australian and international authorities. In positioning readers to share her views, she makes purposeful use of tone, which shifts from conveying feelings of frustration to indicating serious consideration of the evidence, then to expressing feelings of relief and pleasure as she affirms the benefits of being on the beach. The photographs included in the article support the writer's argument and also accord with the shift in tone; the first image, of children watching television, shows only their backs, while the second image, of children playing on a beach, shows happy faces.

Smith's personal experiences and knowledge of parenting young children allows her to connect strongly with her audience who, as readers of the *Child Monthly* magazine, are likely also to be parents of young children and to have been in similar situations. Such readers will find it easy to relate to the familiar descriptions of challenging times involving 'arguments and squabbling' and 'constant demands for attention'. Even for other readers, these phrases create strong negative images of discord and tension, inviting sympathy and also raising the question of how these challenges might be resolved. The reference to an article in the previous issue of the magazine also creates a sense of a shared readership and common concerns, encouraging readers to share Smith's view of children's needs.

Authority figures and statistics lend objectivity and substance to the article, inclining the reader to perceive its argument as stronger and more compelling than a purely personal point of view. Citing government organisations such as the Department of Health and Human Services in the US and the Australian Bureau of Statistics gives the quoted figures credibility and authority. Moreover, Smith guides the reader's response to these figures through emotive terms such as 'alarming' and the emphasis created by italics in the phrase '4.5 hours a day of TV *and* … over an hour a day playing video games'. This leads the reader to feel increasingly anxious about the dominance of technology in children's lives. Smith's rhetorical questions also imply to the reader that sport, reading and homework should be priorities, which most readers would agree with, but that these are largely neglected due to the amounts of screen time reported.

Throughout the first half of the article, Smith creates an idea of time spent in front of a screen being wasted time, and even detrimental to children. In the photograph of children watching television, we see only their backs; they are not shown to be responding physically to what they watch, and the room they sit in lacks any visible objects for play or stimulation (such as toys or books). The blank TV screen suggests they could be watching any program at all, and they would engage in the same immobile and mindless behaviour.

Smith does acknowledge some benefits of young children using computers or tablets, showing that her viewpoint is balanced and reasoned rather than extreme or excessively emotional. Yet these are followed by an account of what is lacking in such activities. The phrase 'totally dormant' in relation to the senses of taste and smell suggests a dismissal of screen-based technologies; the idea of being 'dormant' also connects with the image of stationary children watching the television. In this way,

Smith creates an impression of digital learning as inadequate even as an educating tool, leading to individuals who are somehow inert or not fully developed.

The shift in tone towards the end of the article coincides with Smith's resolution of many of these anxieties, enabling the reader to share in Smith's feelings of 'relief'. This shift in tone is brought about by an increased use of adjectives with positive associations, such as 'soft', 'cool' and 'fresh'. These words convey a pleasurable state of wellbeing that readers would find appealing and desirable. The attractive imagery of the natural world contrasts strongly with the negative ideas that Smith associates with the use of technologies, such as 'dormant' senses or children being 'obese'. This contrast of ideas is even more explicit in the descriptions of her own children's behaviour, which on the beach is now 'content' rather than 'cranky' as it was when the children were constrained to indoor activities.

The photograph of children on the beach also contrasts effectively with the photograph of children indoors watching television. We now see the children's happy faces, and they are clearly engaged in physical activity as well as interacting positively with one another (rather than arguing and squabbling). The caption encapsulates the positive message of the image and of the article's conclusion, which links play and learning. The kind of learning possible through digital technology is made to seem inadequate by comparison with that possible on a beach. The language becomes more poetic and evocative in words such as 'tenacious' and 'eking', suggesting a mini biology lesson to reinforce the positive idea of learning in a natural environment.

Smith concludes with an affirmative, optimistic tone – 'here's looking forward to a long summer' – again in contrast to the article's opening, which looked regretfully backwards. She ends with inclusive language ('all of our lives'), strengthening readers' sense of shared experiences and hopes and leading them also to share her point of view on the kinds of experiences and activities that are best for young children.

Sample response 21: Don't ban the exam

In an edition of *Learning Now*, Bronwyn Leigh responds to calls to eradicate exams for students in Year 12. She uses a calm and often conversational tone to argue that when exams are used in conjunction with other assessment tools they are a reliable and fair form of assessment and that they should therefore remain in use for Year 12 students. The accompanying image can be seen to support Leigh's claims that exams ensure fairness and equality in a way that other forms of assessment generally do not.

The first two sentences of Leigh's article present exams as something daunting. The word 'exams' isolated in a sentence by itself works to mirror the isolation Leigh claims that she herself felt when sitting exams as a student; its isolation also emphasises and confirms Leigh's claim that exams have 'struck fear into generations of students'. It is in an exam that many people feel vulnerable and alone so Leigh's acknowledgement of how many feel about exams allows virtually all readers – 'generations' of them – to initially empathise with her views, despite the fact that the title of her article clearly supports the continued use of exams. Leigh's conversational tone, and her use of terms like 'perhaps' and 'I'm not so sure', also present her as a reasonable and fairly typical person, despite the fact that her biographical details at the conclusion of the article indicate that she has been an academic for over thirty years. This tone, along with later, more obviously colloquial expressions like 'meltdown', 'cramming' and 'zilch', helps to position her as someone who understands what life is like for a wide range of people and therefore encourages readers to be more inclined to value her judgement.

Although Leigh does present her views in a reasonably approachable way, she is not averse to deflating the views of those who present opposing viewpoints, questioning their authority while bolstering her own. Her reference to some opponents as mere 'commentators' who could in fact be anyone who has an opinion about exams as a form of assessment, regardless of whether or not they are qualified on the matter, positions readers to be wary of alternative views. Similarly, the use of the verb 'push' when referring to the 'push to eradicate exams' suggests that her opponents are forcibly proposing an idea rather than advocating a model that should logically evolve. Furthermore, the suggestion that readers should be able to 'guess' the claims made against exams implies that such claims are mostly clichéd and, as she proves, thanks to her years of 'experience as both a student and an educator', easily overturned. In contrast to her own claims of experience, and her assertion that exams have been in place 'since the mid-nineteenth century', Leigh implies that the move to 'abandon' exams is a form of recklessness. Her matter-of-fact statement that, 'like it or not', exams are relevant to everyday life, and her accompanying examples of situations in which both a doctor and a teacher would appear incompetent, position the reader to fear the consequences of a society whose professionals have not had to do exams during their training. No reader would want to be the 'bloodied, distraught accident victim' whose doctor could not respond immediately and effectively to the crisis. This sense of fear is carried through to Leigh's concern about the lack of equality that assessment without exams would produce. She acknowledges that a thesis could facilitate the development of important skills; however, Leigh suggests that impartially marking these 'highly individual pieces of research and writing' is fraught with difficulty and open to abuse. These concerns could easily alarm readers of *Learning Now* who, being interested in education matters, would be disinclined to support a system that is readily exploited.

The accompanying image depicting long rows of empty desks and chairs positioned in an exam setting reinforces Leigh's initial recollections of exams as producing a sense of isolation in students. However, it ultimately works to promote Leigh's desire for fairness and equality. The fact that the tables and chairs are identical symbolises the ways that exams also work to promote parity. The desks might well be blank – much like Leigh's mind was when she initially opened exam papers years ago – however, this also connotes potential and the possibility of a renewed response to an exam situation and exam material. The strong, straight lines of the furniture also highlight the weight Leigh places on exams as being a serious endeavour and as essential to assessment rigour. And, although there are numerous tables and chairs depicted here, the fact that they are relatively inexpensive items of furniture helps to support Leigh's claim that exams are inexpensive to run, unlike multiple theses which many schools would be unable to properly resource and staff.

Sample response 22: Betta fish

Writing for her personal blog, Soto employs an outraged and admonishing tone in criticising pet shops' inhumane treatment of tropical fish, with the ultimate aim of convincing readers to boycott such establishments. The accompanying graphic, showing the proportion of fish deaths following capture, is similarly critical.

Soto firmly opposes the 'horrible conditions' in which tropical fish are kept, a position she has come to following her personal experience of attempting to purchase a Betta fish for her son. She opens with this emotive anecdote, describing the 'distressing sight' of sick and dead fish, and her son's 'trembling voice' as he asked after their welfare. She thus positions herself as an ordinary citizen so alarmed by what she has witnessed that she has been moved to create a blog post about it in protest. Given that her readers are presumably primarily other parents, the upset of the writer and her small son is intended to be relatable and to arouse sympathy.

From the outset, Soto expresses her anger that such an injustice is being perpetrated against innocent creatures in a vehement tone and with firm declarative statements – for example, 'I am *livid*'. The use of italics here emphasises the emotive word, encouraging readers to share the emotion. She details, through evocative imagery, the various transgressions she saw inflicted on tropical fish by a chain pet shop: each fish was in a 'tiny plastic cup' with 'murky water', 'practically stacked on top of each other' in 'plastic prisons'. This language is designed to arouse readers' concern and indignation, appealing to their sense of empathy and justice by vividly evoking a detailed image of the fishes' plight. The accompanying graphic seeks to reinforce these feelings by depicting staggering statistics ('only 1 in 9' fish survive capture long enough to be purchased) alongside dead-eyed cartoon fish. The images of fish skeletons underscore the repercussions of inadequate care and aim to create a sense of alarm in the reader, potentially also evoking readers' guilt if they themselves have purchased ill-treated fish from a pet shop.

Soto links the depiction of animal cruelty to pet shops and their workers, providing readers with a clear target for their outrage. The few staff who work in the particular pet shop Soto visited are depicted as indifferent to the harm being inflicted on the animals in their care – 'the employee just shrugged' – and as having 'absolutely zero knowledge' about how to properly care for Bettas, leading readers to question why these employees are working in this profession at all. The use of a rhetorical question – 'how can a company claim to love animals when their fish are dying …?' – to denigrate companies that employ such people and do not have processes in place to care for animals alerts readers to the institutional failure of such establishments. Soto notes that the issue is 'systemic', and repeatedly makes the point that the reason for this is the company's prioritisation of money over animal welfare. This characterisation of pet shop owners as selfish, cruel and greedy paints an extremely negative picture of them, thus priming readers to be prepared to boycott pet shops without concern about the possible effects on their owners or staff. The use of quotation marks around the words 'not in today' further subtly suggests possible deceit on the part of the shop owner or the staff member, inclining the reader to view them as villainous.

Moreover, Soto characterises the supposed apathy expressed by the employees as representative of society's general disregard for environmental and animal welfare issues; she decries those who 'have gone in and purchased fish with absolutely no idea how to care for them' and exclaims, with an air of condescension, 'Fish feel pain, people!' Again her target is her reader's sense of empathy, which she hopes to direct towards action to protect poorly treated animals. She also aims to educate readers who might not view the issue as particularly important by emphasising the fishes' suffering and encouraging readers to imagine themselves in the place of the fish: 'Imagine being trapped …'

By closing the argument with a call to action, Soto intends to leave readers with a sense of urgency to bring about change. While she momentarily considers an individual response to the problem by suggesting that she would 'buy their whole stock of Bettas so I could rescue them', she quickly counters this – and thus implies her readers should also – by noting that this would only further the cycle of suffering. The call to action she wants to leave readers with is for her 'friends and followers' to join her boycott of pet shops. The use of the inclusive 'we' towards the end of the post further encourages a communal, widespread response to the issue.

Sample response 23: Bookless libraries

Principal Petrov Price's blog solicits support for his intention to remove physical books from the Romeo Road school library and replace them with a digital library. His approach is both firm and gentle, asserting the need for change while anticipating and appreciating the distress this will cause some members of the school community. The confident yet compassionate tone positions readers to feel that the school's future is in good hands, so they should support his plan.

With a structure that places his main contention early in the blog, Price first builds rapport with his audience, priming them to accept the argument, and then provides supporting evidence designed to cement readers' support. The main reasons he presents, all supported with examples, include: moving the school into the twenty-first century; providing students with simpler and more comprehensive access to knowledge and information; reducing costs; freeing up valuable 'real estate' on school premises; and improved hygiene. Price presents all these reasons as being part of his duty of care for 'our school and, most importantly, our students', intending to elicit feelings of group loyalty as well as respect for the principal, further inclining readers to accept his proposal. The admission that the school is 'facing some difficult questions' in the digital age indicates honesty and further evidences the school's commitment to improving facilities for its students and community.

Supporting Price's argument, the design of the blog adds a sense of reassuring authenticity intended to make readers feel that the ideas in 'From the Principal's Corner' are in their best interests. The school logo is likely to prompt a feeling of familiarity in the intended audience (the school community) and will remind readers that they are all part of the same, well-defined, supportive group. Additionally, the text-based navigation map leading to the blog shows that this community's (and thus the principal's) priority is to provide its students with clear, direct, reliable access to information. This underscores the blog's central assertion and encourages readers to believe in Price's argument.

The principal's tone is friendly, candid, sensible, concerned and confident throughout. It is established early in the blog with his anecdote about personal childhood feelings and memories connected with libraries, linked to his current beliefs about information access. This warm tone, the first-person voice (a common element of the blog genre) and inclusive language ('our school', 'our efforts') combine to create a caring and relatable persona. Price's early declaration of his love of libraries is aimed at indicating to his audience that his is an unbiased opinion, showing that he is reasonable, genuine and trustworthy because he has a predisposition to identify closely with (rather than contest or dismiss) those who might object to his proposition. This is intended to incline those initially opposed to the idea to accept his argument. His conciliatory but firm approach is also echoed in his assertion that 'it's controversial, sure – but it's not *that* controversial', respecting yet resisting any disagreement.

Another central strategy used by Price is his appeal to being modern and up to date. He emphasises the idea of a digital future and the school's record of embracing change ('we have since led the way in adopting new technologies'), and he provides specific examples of such changes in paragraph 5. He impels his audience to recognise that digitising what was once paper-based is 'about making information as quickly, easily and widely accessible as possible', and the repetition of this idea throughout aims to strengthen its impact on and influence over his audience. He urges the school to recognise that 'the world is changing', appealing to the fear that Romeo Road could be left behind and, similarly, appealing to fairness and justice in making sure his students are equipped for their futures. Enhancing his appeal to modernity, Price shapes his language to draw the maximum audience attention and empathy, positioning them to support his argument. His rhetorical questions encourage readers to consider the reality of the situation ('What does the library for the digital age look like?'), while his figures of speech ('close the book on Romeo Road library's dark ages'; 'turn the page on the physical book') soften the impact of his potentially unsettling proposal. Having presented his readers with a problem, Price turns to reason and logic to present his solution as the most sensible and efficient one available: 'we end up having to do it later anyway'.

Price's argument strategies are reinforced by the image that concludes the blog, leaving the audience with a strong visual summation of the text in order to help ensure their support. The hand holding a phone contributes to the sense that efficiency can be successfully integrated with interest and engagement; while the image suggests businesslike practicality, it also conveys a sense of enjoyment. The idea portrayed is not a dry database of texts, but rather an amiable representation of digital libraries, offering a visual experience not unlike 'real' libraries: a friendly-looking assortment of books, accessible at the touch of a finger. This image works to enrich the blog's assertion that digital libraries are not just practical, but the positive way forward.

Sample response 24: Colonising Mars

In her piece for the website Science is Super, writer Natasha O'Meara argues that humanity should attempt to colonise Mars. O'Meara writes for a general audience that is interested in and broadly knowledgeable about science, but not necessarily familiar with the specific topic of the piece. She employs a slightly humorous and casual tone throughout the piece. She also uses accessible, emotive and inclusive language, appeals to authority and expert opinion, an anecdote and a list structure to position readers to side with her point of view. The article also includes an image that highlights the possibilities of space colonisation.

The article is structured as a listicle, a common format for online texts. O'Meara uses this structure to segment her main points to make it easier for a general audience, who might not know much about the topic, to digest. This structure also allows the article to use a clickbait title to encourage readers to read to the end of the article. By structuring her points from least to most impactful, O'Meara seeks to keep readers invested and curious about her arguments. This structure also encourages readers who are not persuaded by her first or second points to continue reading until the end of the piece, as they will likely be intrigued to find out why the third reason might 'surprise' them.

Near the beginning of her piece, O'Meara refers to the 'greatest minds of their age', mentioning Stephen Hawking and Carl Sagan as prominent figures who have supported colonising Mars. This primes readers to accept the validity of her arguments; by appealing to the authority of prominent scientific figures, O'Meara suggests that her points are supported by experts and based on scientific consensus, lending them legitimacy. Readers, especially the audience the article is targeted at who are unlikely to be intimately familiar with the subject matter, are expected to feel reluctant to disagree with people who they know are far more knowledgeable about the feasibility of colonising Mars.

Throughout her piece, O'Meara frequently uses emotive language that conveys a sense of urgency. She describes the 'necessity' of a Mars colonial project, referring to it as not just 'a flight of fancy or a project for the distant future', but a 'vital step for humanity to take'. This framing of her argument encourages the reader to view colonising Mars as inevitable, and thus not worth arguing against. It also stresses the importance of this project; the use of extreme language such as 'necessity' and 'vital' is intended to encourage readers to view colonising Mars as something that must be done for the sake of scientific advancement.

The article also frequently appeals to the reader's self-interest, stressing the benefits of Mars for humanity. O'Meara's third point in particular, which the article's headline emphasises, focuses on the material benefits to Earth right now. She argues that 'the benefits are undeniable' and that 'advancements in one area invariably benefit many others'. This encourages readers to view conquering Mars as likely to materially benefit their own lives. O'Meara supports these arguments with her anecdote about the invention of the microwave, illustrating her point about how scientific progress can improve people's living conditions. Here, too, O'Meara uses language that frames these conclusions as self-evident, implying that readers should agree with her and would be foolish not to.

O'Meara also appeals to a sense of fear in the audience, arguing that 'the future of our species could depend' on the colonisation of Mars. By framing her argument in these terms, O'Meara suggests that not supporting the colonisation of Mars could have dire consequences for the human species, aiming to evoke fear in the reader as this is something they are likely to want to avoid.

The article is accompanied by an image, which serves to further support O'Meara's contention. The astronaut faces away from the camera, obscuring any identifying features. This suggests that colonising Mars shouldn't be seen as any individual person's mission, but rather be treated as a collective goal for all of humanity to pursue. It also encourages readers to project themselves onto the image, metaphorically seeing themselves as the intrepid spacefarer ready to conquer foreign planets, regardless of their background. This helps the article appeal to a wide range of readers and to stir their spirit of adventure and desire for advancement. The image is in black and white, again removing identifying characteristics. This also lends the image a historical quality, reinforcing the impression that the mission to colonise Mars isn't just a recent consideration, but has been a goal pursued by humanity for a long time. The image frames the astronaut in silhouette against a seemingly hostile background, and the astronaut's dominance of the frame suggests humanity overcoming the treacherous terrain of Mars. O'Meara's use of the term 'Manifest Destiny' supports this, evoking romanticised imagery of intrepid explorers braving a new world. The human-made structures in the background suggest that humanity colonising Mars is an achievable goal and that to some extent the process has already begun. The image's placement at the beginning of the article reinforces this, priming readers to accept the inevitability of interstellar colonisation.

O'Meara concludes her piece with a rhetorical question, asking of the reader 'So why wait?' The rhetorical question is intended to imply to readers that there isn't a good response; there *is* no reason to wait. By ending her piece with this rhetorical question, O'Meara encourages readers to consider the arguments they have read, keeping them thinking about the topic of colonising Mars with the sense that colonisation is both inevitable and the logical way forward.

Sample response 25: Vegan shoes

In an article in a lifestyle magazine, Tanner Bowden argues that vegan shoes are not necessarily sustainable. Bowden injects nuance into the debate, suggesting that sustainable leather is a complicated issue with no simple answers, by providing a balanced discussion with evidence from different perspectives. He uses a conversational tone to build rapport with his audience of young, environmentally conscious readers. Bowden also uses an explanatory tone to explain the harmful impacts of leather production, as well as sustainable innovations, citing real-world examples to support his arguments.

Bowden begins by both establishing his argument and building rapport with his audience. The first line, 'I have beef with vegan shoes', is snappy and humorous, and incorporates the youthful slang term 'beef', setting up a casual tone that suggests the writer is on the same level as his readers. The opening line, in conjunction with the title, also clearly point to the direction of Bowden's argument, that 'If You Think Your Vegan Shoes Are Saving the Planet, You're Wrong'.

Bowden also builds rapport with readers by positioning himself as environmentally conscious, a stance they are likely to share. While the title hooks readers with the confrontational statement 'You're Wrong' to think vegan shoes are sustainable, Bowden quickly softens this point. For example, he describes vegans as 'heroes' who are 'literally saving the world' and incorporates a personal anecdote about trying a vegan diet as proof that he respects vegans. His use of an anecdote and the first person brings in a personal element to help him connect with readers. Returning to his opening point, Bowden states 'my problem is not with vegans – it's with vegan shoes'. This shift, combined with Bowden's earlier effusive support for veganism, means that vegan readers may feel assuaged that they are not being attacked, and may therefore be more receptive to his argument.

Bowden then begins incorporating an explanatory tone, educating readers about the sustainability of faux and real leather. One technique he uses is rhetorical questions, such as 'How can a shoe be vegan anyway?' These signpost the topic of the explanation, making it easier for readers to stay engaged. This explanatory tone combines with the conversational tone; for example, Bowden uses brackets for the aside about the ingredients of animal-based glues: '(typically, it's collagen)'. This technique mimics the patterns of informal speech, making the article feel more casual.

Bowden next presents the points of view both in favour of and against vegan shoes, arguing that their sustainability does not have a simple answer. The mention of popular brands (Dr. Martens, Adidas) that sell vegan shoes may interest fashion-conscious readers who read lifestyle magazines, suggesting vegan shoes are a trendy issue they should know about. Bowden argues that whether vegan shoes support 'general sustainability' is a complicated question, introducing a main point: there is no quick fix to leather's sustainability issues. Bowden explains that faux leather is 'essentially … plastic' and includes 'harmful chemicals', impressing on readers its environmental drawbacks.

Since companies ignore these environmental dangers, Bowden suggests that the promotion of faux leather shoes can be 'greenwash[ing]'. However, he still maintains the article's balanced approach by including a counterexample: a quote from the company OluKai, which admits that 'animal-free shoes are not always more "environmentally friendly" by default'. However, Bowden stresses that, while OluKai is forthcoming about the drawbacks of vegan shoes, other brands are not, suggesting that the sustainability of shoes is not only related to their materials but companies' lack of transparency, positioning readers to feel wary and distrustful of them.

Moving on to more 'promising' eco-friendly types of faux leather, Bowden lists examples: 'leather' made of apples, pineapple leaves and mushrooms. He does not explicitly explain how these are more sustainable than synthetic faux leather, relying on his environmentally conscious audience to infer that plant-based materials must be more environmentally friendly. This 'more responsibly' produced vegan leather is illustrated through the image accompanying the article. In the image, a leather shoe is positioned next to mushrooms and 'samples of vegan bio leather', as explained in the caption. The mushrooms are arranged haphazardly, reinforcing their link to the natural world. The juxtaposition of unprocessed natural materials ('mushroom mycelium') with the processed form ('bio leather') and the final end-product (shoes) suggests that plant-based vegan shoes could be the solution to this issue of unsustainable vegan leather. The juxtaposition also lends to the vegan shoes and leather the positive natural associations of the mushrooms. Maintaining the balance of his discussion however, Bowden again presents a counterargument: depending on plant-based faux leather is not practical because there is not enough of it being produced. This encourages readers to consider the nuances of the issue – even eco-friendly leather has drawbacks – and therefore primes them to consider his argument that solely relying upon vegan leather might not be the best way forward for sustainable shoe production.

Having discussed the pros and cons of the different kinds of faux leather, Bowden introduces the topic of whether natural leather is 'really so bad'. On the negative side, Bowden uses repetition, saying that natural leather's production involves 'harmful chemicals'. By paralleling his earlier use of that phrase for faux leather, Bowden suggests that the production of both real and faux leather can have similar downsides. Bowden also uses technical terms like 'glutaraldehyde', supporting the explanatory tone by giving a sense of his knowledge on the issue, which aims to position readers to have faith in his opinion.

On the positive side for natural leather, Bowden mentions that it is a by-product of an already-existing industry (beef), foregrounding practicality. He discusses innovations that may make natural leather 'eco-friendlier', providing the example of Patagonia, including how its shoes are mendable and its cattle-raising practises '[restore] the grasslands and [promote] carbon sequestration'. By detailing the sustainability efforts of this popular brand, Bowden positions readers to think that sustainable natural leather in shoes is deserving of their attention.

Once again, Bowden balances this viewpoint with the practical truth that these methods cannot be used on a large scale, and explicitly reminds readers that the same is true of plant-based faux leather. This suggests that neither plant-based leather nor sustainably sourced natural leather are silver bullets that will fix the environmental impacts of producing shoes.

Bowden links this point to a statement that sums up his argument: 'sustainability is complicated'. This statement acknowledges readers' likely confusion in the face of all these options, before Bowden segues into his conclusion by reminding readers of reasons for 'hope' because 'both vegan and non-vegan footwear is getting more sustainable'. This avoids leaving readers on a despairing note that may make them disengage. Additionally, by summarising his earlier points in this concise way, Bowden leaves readers with clear key points to remember. His final lines, guessing that 'chances are' Adidas and Allbirds' new sustainable shoe 'won't be vegan', bookend the article with mentions of veganism. Ending with one of his key points, that 'vegan' and 'sustainable' are not necessarily synonymous, he leaves readers with the message that they should be sceptical of companies' environmental claims and think carefully about their shoe purchasing choices.

Acknowledgements

Insight Publications thanks the following writers for their contributions to this resource: Samantha Anderson, Laken Ballinger, Anica Boulanger-Mashberg, Sage Napthine-Morrison, Tess Rooney, Olivia Shenken, Alison Tealby, Mariano Trevino and Fabrice Wilmann.

Insight Publications is also grateful to the following individuals and organisations for permission to reproduce copyright material.

Fiona Carruthers and *The Australian Financial Review* for 'Overtourism: why you're the one to blame'.

Wendy Squires and *The Sydney Morning Herald* for 'The jaywalking phone zombie plague is completely out of control'.

Tanner Bowden and *Gear Patrol* for 'If You Think Your Vegan Shoes Are Saving the Planet, You're Wrong'.

Images by Melisa Paredes and Gisela Beer. Other images from iStock and Shutterstock.

The article from *The Conversation*, 'One cat, one year, 110 native animals: lock up your pet, it's a killing machine', was written by Jaana Dielenberg, University Fellow, Charles Darwin University; Brett Murphy, Associate Professor / ARC Future Fellow, Charles Darwin University; Chris Dickman, Professor in Terrestrial Ecology, University of Sydney; John Woinarski, Professor (conservation biology), Charles Darwin University; Leigh-Ann Woolley, Adjunct Research Associate, Charles Darwin University; Mike Calver, Associate Professor in Biological Sciences, Murdoch University; and Sarah Legge, Professor, Australian National University.

The article from *The Conversation*, 'What our love affair with coffee pods reveals about our values', was written by John Rice, Associate Professor in Strategic Management, Griffith University, and Nigel Martin, Lecturer, College of Business and Economics, Australian National University.

Note: Some articles were written in previous years and so may include some dated references.